I0796845

You Bet *Your* Stretch Marks

Abbie Halberstadt

Illustrations by Lindsay Long

HARVEST HOUSE PUBLISHERS
EUGENE, OREGON

Cover design by Faceout Studio, Molly von Borstel
Cover concept, cover illustration (tiger), and interior illustrations by Lindsay Long
Cover illustrations (florals) by Leah Beachy; texture image © natrot / Shutterstock
Interior design by Janelle Coury
Author photo by Jessica Helgesen Photography

For bulk, special sales, or ministry purchases, please call 1-800-547-8979.
Email: CustomerService@hhpbooks.com

You Bet Your Stretch Marks

Published by Harvest House Publishers
Eugene, Oregon 97408
www.harvesthousepublishers.com

ISBN 978-0-7369-8677-9 (hardcover)
ISBN 978-0-7369-8678-6 (eBook)

Library of Congress Control Number: 2024953008

Printed in China

25 26 27 28 29 30 31 32 33 / RDS / 10 9 8 7 6 5 4 3 2 1

To Jennifer. You are the "gone-before" mama-friend of every girl's dreams. Your grammar expertise, your enthusiasm and encouragement, your level-headed good sense—I cherish them all!

Contents

Introduction

Can you tell your children not to SHOUT?!" The angry, decidedly French voice cut through the squawks and shrieks of our two-and-a-half-year-old twin boys, halting my husband, Shaun, and me mid-toy grab.

It was hour twenty-five of a bleary-eyed thirty-hour travel day with ten children in tow, and Titus and Toby were *done*. Done with snacks. Done with gadgets. Done with shows. Done. *Done.* DONE.

I was much too frazzled to notice the similarity at the time, but recalling that Eurostar ride now brings to mind a scene from an episode of *Gilmore Girls* (a series that I cannot recommend wholesale but whose machine-gun dialogue often made me grin). In it, Luke, the crotchety diner owner, tells his long-time crush, Lorelai, that the toy a frantic father is waggling in his child's face won't achieve the desired result because "Choo-Choo Joe" is dead.

That's what it felt like in that moment of intense effort to entertain two little boys who had long since surpassed the limits of their ability to be cooperative human beings. Toys were dead to them. And despite Shaun's and my best impression of some strange two-headed octopus parent (we for sure were using our hands *and* feet), the exhaustion was winning.

But our French train companion was not the least bit interested in how long we'd been traveling, or in our obvious ongoing efforts to distract and quiet the twinbies (our affectionate nickname for our twin boys that distinguishes them from their twin sisters, whom we call the twinsies), or in the fact that our other eight children were doing excellent impressions of considerate humans.

She was interested in silence.

Frankly, Shaun and I were too tired and a bit too stunned by her sudden interjection to come up with, well, anything. We stared at each other in bemusement, a writhing, protesting toddler in each lap, wondering if she expected an actual response.

We quickly found out she did when, hands glued to hips, she shouted (yes, *shouted*), "YOU DO NOT CARE?!"

Shaun smiled wanly and, assuring her we cared very much, scooped up Toby and swayed down the aisle toward the dining cart. I stayed with Titus and the rest of our children, bouncing, shushing, and distracting him—a slightly easier feat without his brother there to pull his hair or take his coloring book.

Perhaps some of you are feeling a bit indignant with our French "friend"? (I'll admit I was.) Perhaps some of you are annoyed at us. (She certainly was.) Perhaps there are even more of you wondering what exactly in the literal wide world could have tempted us to brave so many hours on so many planes, trains, and automobiles with so many children. What could possibly make such an ordeal worth it?

The answer: a forty-five-day trip to Europe we had been planning for four years by the time it finally came to fruition, a trip that had already been canceled once by COVID-19 (if you've read *M Is for Mama*, you'll recall that sad tale). In other words, we were gritting our teeth through a *very* challenging short-term ordeal to be able to partake in a long-awaited adventure. As it so happened, it ended up being an experience that far surpassed even our wildest imaginings in the levels of joy, wonder, discovery, and—yes—difficulty we encountered. When all was said and done, it was *more* than worth it. It was an experience of a lifetime for our whole family.

But in that exact moment of angst and loopy fatigue on the train, it would have been easy to assume we'd made a mistake, to measure the rest of the trip by the reading on our current stress-o-meter, which was surely at the "too much, dummy, turn back" mark.

Except we couldn't turn back. We had spent the previous nine months researching, packing, praying, and planning to get to this very moment. We were all in, and retreat was no longer an option.

Anybody else think this sounds a bit like the entire all-in enterprise we call parenting?

We spend nine months feverishly researching, packing the birthing bag, praying, and planning to get to that moment when we finally make euphoric eye contact for the first time with the slippery soul we've been watching turn our bellies into an alien landscape of fleshy hills and valleys for so long.

And we know, in that moment of exhausted bliss, we are all in, and retreat is no longer an option. (Truly, from the moment of conception, it never was.)

We promise ourselves we will never be anything less than *the most* present, *the most* patient, *the most* invested mama who has ever existed. Because, no matter what we face, it *will* be worth it. How could it not be when holding this new little being is like holding a slice of heaven in our arms?

We mean every word. We do.

And yet, one whole week later, we find ourselves drowning in an existential malaise of adult diapers, upside-down days and nights, milk-stained tees, and quick bites of our husband's leftover toast. It's worth it, we remind ourselves. It's worth doing *the most*.

We begin to hit our newborn stride. We witness that first gassy, lopsided smirk, and our hearts melt like butter left too close to the griddle. We get four uninterrupted hours of sleep for the first time in a month, and we're sure we could cure world hunger with the energy and mental clarity we've achieved.

But then along come toddlerdom, the sassy five-year-old stage, prepubescence, and—oh dear—the dreaded teenage years.

Each stage has the potential to chip away at our resolve to be *the most*, and, although I'm not usually one to blame "society" for all our woes, I'm sad to say moms are much more likely to encounter "French woman on the train" energy than a "trust God, Mama" response when we find ourselves flailing in uncharted, stormy mothering waters.

And so we begin to doubt our wisdom in committing to this child-rearing thing. What if we royally flub the whole business? What if we're remortgaging our house to pay for three kids' worth of therapy in ten years? (If parenting articles are telling it like it is, this will *definitely* be true.) What if that commitment to *the most* was just our mushy hormones lying to us?

What were we thinking?

Well, friends, maybe we were thinking this: "Behold, children are a heritage from the Lord, the fruit of the womb a reward" (Psalm 127:3).

"Behold, children are a heritage from the Lord, the fruit of the womb a reward." (Psalm 127:3)

Maybe we felt the Holy Spirit tapping us on the shoulder one night in the middle of a panic-scroll nursing session that had us convinced we could *never* be enough for this bundle of humanity in our arms and saying, "You can do *the most*, and you will still never be enough. But that's good news. Because I am 'able to do far more abundantly than all that [you] ask or think, according to the power at work within [you]'" (Ephesians 3:20).

Maybe we just need to keep our eyes fixed on the bright horizon like the brave mouse, Reepicheep, in C.S. Lewis's *The Voyage of the Dawn Treader*, and declare with him:

> Where the sky and water meet,
> When the waves grow sweet,
> Doubt not, Reepicheep,

To find all you seek,
There is the utter East.[1]

In other words, there may be a poopy diaper (or three!) at our feet, but there is "strength for today and bright hope for tomorrow"[2] if only we can keep our chins up and our eyes trained on Jesus, the Author and Finisher of our faith.

Even with an eyes-up approach, will we still struggle?

Yep.

Will we stumble and fall?

Of course.

Will it be painful and hard at times?

Without a doubt.

But will it be worth it? For us? For them?

You bet your stretch marks!

Titus Two Perspectives

One objection I've encountered through the years since I began sharing what the Lord has taught me through motherhood goes something like this: "I need to know how her kids turn out as adults before I'll listen to anything this lady says." I get it. I, too, find myself craning my neck to see the "finished product" of my friends' parenting. And while I do have older children, including a legal adult (and another who will join him very soon), I thought it would be valuable to include end-of-chapter contributions from older moms than I who share my conviction that our work matters and is worth the daily investment. I asked thirteen wise, godly, committed mamas whom I get to call friends if they'd share perspectives from their experiences as mothers of adult children. To my delight, they all said yes! Some are authors and speakers. Others are close personal friends. One is my own dear mama. All have beautiful words of encouragement for you from which I know you'll receive so much goodness. Enjoy!

A Titus Two Perspective

SEPTEMBER MCCARTHY

author, podcast host, mother of ten

I still do a head count when we leave the house, sit down at a restaurant, go to church, or shop as a family. I have yet to cut back on how many people I cook for, and I still wake up thinking about every single child I prayed over and laid down to bed every night for the last thirty-two years. Seven of our ten children have moved into adulthood, yet I am still their mother. Are there things I would change? You betcha. Are there things my kids would have wanted me to change? No doubt. But the only good thing about looking back is to see how motherhood changed me, grew me, and stretched me. As my body bears the marks of motherhood, so does the imprint of my commitment to bear down on the hard and holy moments, to give my children life—a full life, with no regrets. Now, living in the abundant fruit of perseverance, holding on to hope, ignoring the naysayers (because they weren't sacrificing sleep, tears, and finances for my children—I was), and leaning in to the biggest and most beautiful thing I have ever done with my life: when God made me a mother.

As a mom to ten amazing and very different children, I am now watching the next generation unfold, currently with twelve grandchildren and counting. I have learned that looking forward and not back is the very thread of hope and help that carried me to this moment in time as a mom. I knew that defining motherhood by a bad moment, a horrible day, or a season of exhaustion would reap nothing but discouragement and despair. I chose to think forward—to watch the women before me who exuded patience and a calm exterior in the face of big (and small) challenges and who raised good and godly children who still love her despite her own insecurities, doubts, or bad mom days. I deliberately made each day its own, creating and re-creating our rhythms until it all came together. Motherhood never looked the same from one day to the next. There wasn't a formula but rather a foundation on which I laid my head to rest every night, along with the lives of my children. I had Jesus, the One who had me and my motherhood. Every time I gave Jesus my children's lives, He gave me new hope for a new day. He gave me a future, which I am now living in the present. I am abundantly blessed and still shaking my head at how God could use my yes to motherhood, each and every time. Now, here I am, with no regrets.

As each chapter in this book unfolds, bearing the fruit of saying yes to motherhood one day at a time, you will read from other seasoned moms, giving you a forward vision to hold on to. Motherhood is reclaimed with words of wisdom, testimonies of help, hope for you, and a new vision for what "can be," rather than what the world may tell us "should be."

As you read the culmination of each story shared, I encourage you to remember the daily choices and surrenders of the hardest days, to bring them to a place of abundant blessing. We have one of the grandest jobs ever—enjoy it.

CHAPTER 1

An Eternal Investment

Did you know "child-free living" is a trending topic in online forums like Reddit and Quora as of the year of our Lord 2025?

This may sound like an odd question with which to kick off the first chapter of a book that seeks to demonstrably assure you that investing well in your children is, indeed, a worthy pursuit.

But hang with me for a minute.

Because I doubt there's a reader who hasn't, for at least the briefest of moments, imagined how different her life would be without her children.

Before you fire off an angry email saying, "Not me, Halberstadt! I would never!" keep in mind I didn't say our imaginings had to be positive (or negative, depending on your perspective). I've conjured images of a child-free existence more than once in an attempt to grapple with the contemptuous attitude toward children I've encountered in internet threads like those I just mentioned. In a viral video, comedian Chelsea Handler boasted of her ability to do "whatever the #$%* I want," including references to ingesting cannabis when she wakes early, going back to sleep until noon, and pursuing other forms of "entertainment" I'll pass on mentioning. For the sake of intellectually grasping the appeal of the completely self-focused existence Handler describes, I've contemplated the prospect of Saturday lie-ins, vacations on a whim, and food prep for only one.

But not once have I reached the conclusion my life would be more joyful, more fulfilled, or more character-rich without children in it.

Easier?

Well, that, my friends, is a horse of a different color.

If you've read *Hard Is Not the Same Thing as Bad*, you're fully briefed on my stance on easy versus worthwhile. (And if you haven't, you might be surprised, given the title, to know I don't think the two are mutually exclusive.)

The thing is, we don't just encounter "child regret" in the questionable morass of anonymous misery one-upmanship that overflows these message boards. Sometimes it comes from a much more unsettling source.

The Children Are Not The Problem

One morning, as I was doing some work in my "girl cave" (my pet name for the closest thing I have to an office), I received an email from a mom who was struggling. This, in itself, is not uncommon. In fact, I would say 50 percent of the messages I receive could be filed under the "struggling moms" tab. Parenting is challenging, and we all have questions.

But this email was different. The writer mentioned listening to a podcast in which I was elucidating just the premise of this book—that children, while capable of stretching us to our limits (and beyond), are worth the effort.

She let me know that, while in most cases she would agree with me, her own circumstances precluded such a conclusion.

She wasn't a "regular mom." She was a mom struggling with disabilities. She didn't share a diagnosis, but she detailed a many-years-long fight against symptoms of fatigue and debilitating pain. Her circumstances would be (and had been) challenging for a single person without children.

But they were infinitely more so now that she did have children.

So, why did she have children at all? Well, because she got married, and that was the next logical step. And also because the women at her church had told her that it would be worth it. That no one ever regretted children. That she would never get to the end of her life and wish she'd spent more time on herself and less with her children.

I think we've all heard similar sentiments, and while I wholeheartedly believe the seed of truth in them is robust and fruitful, they also can ring a bit hollow when we're in a place of overwhelm.

Sometimes we need to take a moment to remember those in-the-trenches years and find our compassion. As I read on, though, I felt my sympathy for her struggles begin to morph into concern.

You see, she wasn't just messaging me to ask for prayer or to get advice or even to vent. She was writing because she believed I'd overlooked something crucial to the "kids are worth it" conversation.

The missing element? The fact that no one is telling women with disabilities they shouldn't have children. She thought I was just the one to remedy the problem.

She was a Christian, she said. And before children, she'd had the ability to rest and recharge enough to be a blessing to members of her church community by making them meals or visiting the elderly at home.

She considered these worthwhile efforts (as do I), and she resented the fact that her very small children's constant neediness gobbled up the scraps of energy she managed to conserve on her best days, leaving her with nothing to offer anyone beyond her own household.

She acknowledged her husband was selfless and giving, helpful around the house, and patient with the children. She noted her church was supportive—often chipping in to help with chores and childcare. The "problem" was her children. Their needs were constant. She could no longer recover for several days at a time to regather her strength. She couldn't be her best self. They were whiny and unappreciative of what little energy she did have to offer.

She was convinced the very people to whom she had ministered in the past and who now served her in her time of need had bamboozled her into an enterprise on which she should have never embarked.

And she wanted me to set the record straight. Motherhood is only "worth it" for the able-bodied, the pain-free.

Perhaps most worrisome of all was her contention that, whereas children are not guaranteed to receive Christ, and are therefore (according to her) dubious beneficiaries of our care and effort, people who already are Christians are worth the sacrifice.

Friends, I recognize this is a unique (and biblically twisted) perspective, but it speaks to some underlying assumptions many of us can harbor—regardless of the obstacles we face in motherhood—without even realizing it.

Just a few to consider:

- Children "keep us" from ______________.
- We would be better Christians if only we didn't have these babies at our feet getting "in the way."
- Children are not as worthy of our best efforts as adults are (because grown-ups can better recognize and appreciate what we have to offer).
- The older ladies who tell us it's worth it just don't "get it" anymore.

Convinced I needed to at least try to break through this desperately unhappy woman's determined narrative of "buyer's remorse," I emailed her back, expressing my compassion for her struggles and gently reminding her that her children would not always be so time-consuming and that, were she to see them as a worthy investment of even her smallest kernels of energy, she would, I wholeheartedly believed, begin to see the fruit of her efforts.

The Most Important Work

Shaken by the interaction, I asked my online community for feedback from moms with disabilities. Did they agree with the notion that a "children are worth it" stance needed to come with an "unless you're disabled" caveat? Or did they find the energy expended on their children well spent, even if it looked different from what their friends with fewer physical struggles experienced?

To a woman, the responses were unanimous.

Yes, it's *hard work*. And much more so when we battle migraines or autoimmune diseases or mobility issues. But none of these factors change the fact that the precious children God has given us merit every bit of our energy and more. That shepherding their eternal souls, far from pointless and inferior, is the best use of our time in this season of having children at home.

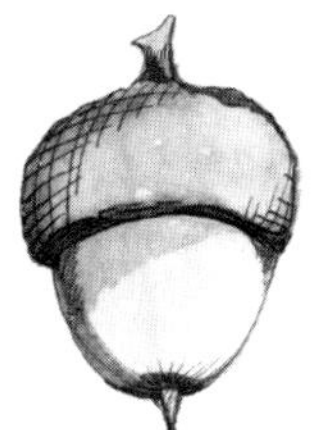

The precious children God has given us merit every bit of our energy and more... shepherding their eternal souls, far from pointless and inferior, is the best use of our time in this season of having children at home.

Their responses immediately brought to mind this iconic quote from Dr. John Trainer: "Children are not a distraction from more important work. They are the most important work."

Of course, we know, from a biblical perspective, the most important work is truly to "love the Lord your God with all your heart and with all your soul and with all your mind...And a second is like it: You shall love your neighbor as yourself" (Matthew 22:37, 39). But a perspective that skips over the closest neighbors we will ever have (namely, the eternal souls who sleep in bed with us or a few rooms away) to run eagerly toward the ones on the other side of our fenced yard will rob us of a "first things (people) first" approach to loving our family well.

Perhaps one of the staunchest proponents of children as a worthy investment I know—even amidst intense physical struggle—is my friend Taylor Brenner, whom I also referenced in *Hard Is Not The Same Thing as Bad*. Taylor began her arduous journey to motherhood in a wheelchair as a foster (then adoptive) mama. Her inability to walk resulted from a cliff-jumping incident gone horribly wrong. The agony she has endured to complete daily tasks staggers the imagination. And yet she has responded to the opportunity to mother a sibling group, who have become children of her heart if not of her blood, with the kind of steadfast commitment to excellence that both inspires and convicts me. Hearing the joy, pride, and dogged commitment with which she speaks of her children—all of whom come with struggles of their own due to the circumstances that necessitated their foster placement—always spurs me on to be more intentional with my own blessings.

And then? The Lord blessed Taylor with a miraculous pregnancy, which doctors had told her was all but impossible after her accident. But even that came with significant challenges—namely, hyperemesis gravidarum (a condition that causes excessive, repetitive vomiting for multiple months throughout pregnancy, sometimes even leading to hospitalization for dehydration) and a complicated delivery due to her many surgeries and pelvic floor instability after the accident.

And yet? I can only imagine the look of disbelief Taylor would give me were I to have the audacity to even imply that, because of her health challenges, she *shouldn't* be a mother.

Her incredulity would be fully warranted.

A Regrettable Regret

Of course, in a culture that champions self-love as the highest form of enlightenment, it should come as no surprise that some would deny the truth that "children are always worth it"—not just for those who suffer physical limitations but for anyone who wakes up one morning and concludes, "You know what? I just don't like being a parent. Sure wish I could have a do-over because I would choose to skip it, given the choice."

Think I'm exaggerating?

Sadly, no.

In a *Time* article entitled "The Parents Who Regret Having Children" (which popped up as "recommended news" on my phone one day), the electively childless author made a case for destigmatizing an attitude of remorse for having had children.[1]

Intrigued, I read it from start to finish, determined to understand a mindset I'd previously encountered only in fringe emails, angsty message boards, or one-off newscast invitations to debate a "child-free lifestyle advocate." Surely, in committing myself fully to this article, I would uncover some shred of relatability or have the briefest "aha" moment of clarity. Surely, the sole reason for its existence couldn't be so brazen as "kids are hard, and I wanted more time to myself."

I was wrong.

In each example in the article, the anonymous regretful parents asserted the primary reasons for their disappointments stemmed from the feeling of having "lost out." Sleep, advanced degrees, free time—all seemed tantalizingly out of reach after becoming parents, and all the more to be mourned.

One mother, who made it clear she would "never ever" make the choice to be one again if afforded a second chance, pointed out her own childhood was affluent and carefree, which led her to believe her experience as a parent should be the same.

When it wasn't, she felt duped.

Citing the endless mothering duties of chauffeur, chef, psychiatrist, physician, confidant (and so on) as the cause for her grief, she made it clear that, though she never wanted her children to know of her remorse, she felt her time would have been better spent doing none of those things.

The author of the article was quick to note that, while parents feel hesitant to express such thoughts out loud (for fear of social censure), there are more of them than we think, and they deserve to be heard without any shame strings attached.

Who Is at the Wheel?

Here's the thing, friends.

If we enter parenthood expecting uninterrupted access to our childless "privileges," we *will* be disillusioned after a single week of sleepless nights and diaper changes on repeat.

If we engage in one of the most virtuously self-denying undertakings with "Self" at the wheel, in the passenger seat, and taking up every spot in the back of the minivan (or stylish SUV, if we've promised ourselves we will never stoop to "minivan mama" status), we will resent any little stowaways on board our Craft of Conceit.

If, however, we approach the monumental task of nurturing, protecting, and helping shape the bedrock beliefs of *another human being* with enough humility to admit we might (just *might*) receive more, learn more, grow more, laugh more, cry more, and, yes, *love more* (not less) in the process, there's a very good chance we'll be right.

If, however, we approach the monumental task of nurturing, protecting, and helping shape the bedrock beliefs of ***another human being*** *with enough humility to admit we might (just* ***might****) receive more, learn more, grow more, laugh more, cry more, and, yes,* ***love more*** *(not less) in the process, there's a very good chance we'll be right.*

That's the nature of expectations. We so often find that which we seek.

Now, I'm not one to "manifest." To do so would be to contradict clear instruction from God's Word. In a culture inundated with memes about "claiming our destiny" or "trusting the universe to bring the success we deserve," James 4:15 counters with a sober-minded right hook: "*If the Lord wills*, we will live and do this or that" (emphasis mine).

However, Jesus says, "Let the little children come to Me, and do not hinder them! For the kingdom of heaven belongs to such as these," (Matthew 19:14 BSB). It is not ungodly manifesting to agree with Him by acknowledging the fact that children hold great worth as image-bearers of our Creator and are and will be worthy investments of our time and resources.

That's the kind of "name it, claim it" energy I can get behind!

It's a fact reiterated in Psalm 127 (which I mentioned in the introduction): "Blessed is the man who fills his quiver with [children]! He shall not be put to shame when he speaks with his enemies in the gate" (verse 5).

Perhaps, then, it is not our offspring who have robbed us of, well, anything. Perhaps it is a mindset of impending disappointment that steals our joy and replaces our vision for legacies built with regret for leisure time lost.

Human but Hopeful

Before you snap this book shut, convinced I must never have experienced any despondency as a parent, let me be clear that neither my husband, Shaun, nor I are exempt from parenting burnout. More to the point, we're perfectly capable of falling prey to an attitude of self-focus that narrows our view to one of petulance at missing out on certain experiences.

Perhaps, then, it is not our offspring who have robbed us of, well, anything. Perhaps it is a mindset of impending disappointment that steals our joy and replaces our vision for legacies built with regret for leisure time lost.

We have squabbled over whose turn it is to stay home while the other has a night out with friends, been bad-tempered when a hike with complaining

INVESTMENT IN ETERNAL SOULS IS THE
WORTHIEST PURSUIT BEYOND OUR
PRIMARY CALLING TO LOVE GOD
FIRST—IS, IN FACT, A NATURAL OUTFLOW OF
THAT LOVE FOR HIM.

children takes three times longer than it "should," and sighed with relief as the last child's "night night" fades into the corners of a blissfully quiet house.

In other words, we are human. We experience periodic exhaustion and disbelief that a particularly onerous stage has dragged on longer than we dreamed possible, same as you.

But we have also gasped in delight as a minutes-old baby claims our hearts with a simple cocooning of our pinky fingers in her feather-soft hands. We have felt our chests swell fair to bursting as our six-year-old hoists one of his twin toddler brothers on his back to save tender feet from "pokies" in the grass. We have joyfully witnessed an entirely unique bearer of the *imago Dei* blossom as a young adult in his God-given interests, talents, and giftings.

And we have often locked eyes, shaking our heads in wonder at the incredible privilege of *getting* to raise our children.

And so, my friends, despite a pendulum that seems to be swinging steadily in the "ew, pass" direction when it comes to children, I say it again: Investment in eternal souls is the worthiest pursuit beyond our primary calling to love God first—is, in fact, a natural outflow of that love for Him. And if the Lord sees fit to grant us eternal souls to shepherd in the form of children here on earth, the only way we will miss out is if we fail to recognize that we will take neither "me time" nor nicer furniture nor "trips of a lifetime" nor spotless car interiors to heaven with us, but instead only those everlasting souls whom God calls to Himself, at least in part, through our steadfast witness of love and instruction in His ways.

A Titus Two Perspective

LISA JACOBSON
author, founder of Club31Women.com,
mother of eight

Strange to think your whole world can dramatically change in just one day.

But that's how it was when our sweet Avonléa was born.

I'd gone in for a routine appointment at thirty-four weeks when suddenly—and quite unexpectedly—they whisked me away for an emergency C-section. I say "unexpectedly" because I'd given birth to four other healthy children, ages six and under, and this was our fifth child. I had no reason to think this pregnancy or birth would be any different.

Yet this experience would become unbelievably different—in every way.

Even the medical staff was mystified, and it wasn't until days later that we learned our daughter had suffered a massive stroke in utero, an extremely rare event. The result was severe brain damage, and the doctor's prognosis was grim: "She will never walk, talk, or even know you as her parents...if she lives at all." After delivering those dizzying words, our lives became a blur of brain surgeries, tube feedings, IVs, and hospitalizations.

And that first doctor was right. Avonléa doesn't have the use of her legs or the left side of her body; she relies on a wheelchair. Yet he was mistaken about the rest. She recently celebrated her twenty-fourth birthday, and she's quite the chatterbox. She definitely knows and loves me, her daddy, and everyone else in her small world.

As you read our story, you may be thinking, "Oh no, I could never go through that." And I get it. That certainly would have been my response before Avonléa. Yet here we are, by the grace of God.

Or it might be that you're only starting on a similar journey, and all you can see are the hard and the heartbreak you're facing. I hear you and trust the Lord to uphold you as He has us.

Plus, let me encourage you with something else the doctor neglected to mention: Avonléa is *a gift*. She has brought more love, compassion, and laughter into our lives than we ever could've imagined.

We have learned so much—and our entire family has grown immensely—in our care for her. We've had to grow in selflessness because her every need is right before us. We've learned to lighten up because you can't stay too serious when she repeats the same silly story (for the hundredth time). And watching this girl overcome the many hurdles and hardships day after day helps put our own "problems" in perspective.

I include "our entire family" because Avonléa's story hasn't changed only my life; it has significantly affected all our children—from her four older siblings down to her three young brothers. To the point that a woman recently questioned her next younger brother, age twenty-two, about his experience. She bluntly asked, "Do you ever regret...or resent...having a sister with such severe special needs?"

Admittedly, I was anxious to hear what he'd say about having a sibling who has required our family to give up so much for her sake. He paused thoughtfully and then answered, "To be honest, I've never thought of Avonléa as anything but *a gift*."

And he's right. She's truly our unexpected gift from God.

The Narrative

A WORLDLY RESPONSE TO "WORTH IT"	A BIBLICAL RESPONSE TO "WORTH IT"
Views the ways children change her life as a negative thing	Sees the inevitable changes as opportunities to grow and improve
Considers a woman's impact and worth lessened by the arrival of children	Recognizes the incredible opportunity for influence afforded by caring for the tiny "neighbors" God has entrusted to her care
Focuses on what "could have been"	Thanks God for the reality of what is, even when it's hard

Action Steps

- Memorize and meditate on Psalm 127:3: "Behold, children are a heritage from the LORD, the fruit of the womb a reward."
- Make a list of three regrets in motherhood. Make a list of three things you enjoy most about motherhood.
- Place sticky notes with the reminder "motherhood is an eternal investment" in high-visibility areas (bathroom mirrors, kitchen sink window, fridge, etc.).

Questions

Do your lists of regrets and enjoyments in motherhood most closely align with the "worldly" or the "biblical" category in our narrative?

Are you more prone to want to go the extra mile for "neighbors" outside your home than the ones who live with you? Why or why not?

What is your daily motherhood mindset? One of investing in eternity, one of surviving the day, or something else entirely?

Prayer

Lord, help us to recognize the attitude we are to emulate when Jesus says, "Let the little children come to Me." May we recognize and value the eternal investment opportunities inherent to raising children, rather than focusing only on the messy or inconvenient aspects of their care. Amen.

CHAPTER 2

When You Walk, Sit, Lie, and Stand

In light of an increasingly child-averse society, don't be surprised if you're mocked both online and in face-to-face interactions as you declare the sacrifice to be an intentional parent both a privilege and a joy. I've personally witnessed scorn in internet forums that label women (me included) who have more than one or two children "breeders," TikTok videos full of references to preborn human babies as "parasites," and even co-workers who thoughtlessly tossed their "condolences" at a father who announced his wife's pregnancy.

And yet, for every blog post or viral video championing the ecstasies of consequence-free promiscuity, traveling the world in kid-free luxury, or living that DINK (Double Income No Kids) life, countering viewpoints do exist—many from secular sources—proclaiming this simple truth, summed up by famous broadcast journalist, Barbara Walters: "I was so busy with a career. It's the age-old problem. And, you know, on your deathbed, are you going to say, 'I wish I spent more time in the office?' No. You'll say, 'I wish I spent more time with my family,' and I do feel that way."[1]

Bill Gates, Oscar De La Hoya, Michael Douglas, and Marc Anthony are just a few more famous individuals who've publicly expressed regrets at becoming too wrapped up in personal pursuits to the detriment of their offspring. Many other famous folks have little to no contact with their children as a result of prioritizing career over family time.

But self-focus to the detriment of our bonds with our children is hardly limited to actors and celebrity authors.

Alexis Ohanian (husband to world-renowned tennis champ Serena Williams and—ironically—co-creator of Reddit, home to some of the most vitriolic child-free threads I've encountered) had this to say on the subject of parental absenteeism: "Do you know the ONE thing I keep hearing from the most successful CEOs? 'I wish I'd spent more time with my kids.' You can have the most successful career in the world and, turns out, that still won't make up for missing time with your kids."[2]

I'd like to stretch this sentiment further to say that it is not merely a generic "time with your kids" that fills this void. After all, if this were true, then "existing in the same room together" would suffice to check this box and assuage this remorse. And while the sense of belonging that comes from simply "being together" may be enough to tide our children over until we have the bandwidth to invest more intentionally, it is no accident that Deuteronomy 6:6-7 (NIV) says, "These commandments that I give you today are to be on your hearts. Impress them on your children. Talk about them when you sit at home and when you walk along the road, when you lie down and when you get up."

To *impress* a concept upon another human being requires not only time but also careful, intentional repetition and modeling. Verse 7 underscores the importance of this concept when it mentions specific activities we do while instructing our children: sitting, walking, lying down, getting up.

Doesn't leave a lot of wiggle room for mentally checking out, does it?

The Lord, through Moses, is establishing the parameters for daily liturgy—a commonplace catechism of worship that requires no church building or rites more sacred than the everyday practices of a family at work and play together.

Let's break it down a bit, shall we?

"These commandments that I give you today are to be on your hearts. Impress them on your children. Talk about them when you sit at home and when you walk along the road, when you lie down and when you get up."
(Deuteronomy 6:6-7 NIV)

The Motions of Motherhood

When you sit: Our family does Bible reading together most mornings at 7:30 a.m. Although, to be fair, not everyone is sitting. The littles are just as likely to be standing on their heads or trotting around under my feet as I make eggs in the kitchen that opens to our living room where we read. We must also often remind the older kids to "sit up" from the somnolent slumps on the couch that characterize many teenagers' posture for the first thirty minutes after they roll out of bed. Regardless of lack of perfect sitting etiquette, this consistent habit is just one example of "impressing" God's ways on our children as we sit.

The same goes for perching on the piano bench next to your child during practice sessions to speak words of life and encouragement (Proverbs 18:21), or sitting beside a child who is doing a lesson on fractions and "being patient with our faces" (as I once heard Sally Clarkson, whom you'll hear from at the end of this chapter, charmingly put it), or sitting on the front porch shelling peas (as I distinctly remember doing at my grandmother's house as a child) while lending godly advice.

When you walk: I have fond childhood memories of evening strolls with my brother, mom, and dad to the tiny municipal airport a mere half mile from our home. As twilight spread like a humid blanket over East Texas nights, the stars would begin to wink their way to life in the dusky sky, and we would flop down on deserted, pebble-strewn runways and gaze upward—the better to comprehend: "The heavens declare the glory of God; the skies proclaim the work of His hands" (Psalm 19:1 BSB).

Or maybe you find yourself charging through a grocery store, squawking toddler straining at the cart's safety belt. As you mentally chant the five necessary items you came for, you also sing "This Little Light of Mine" out loud, both as entertainment for your little one and a reminder (to both her and you) of the opportunity to shine the light of Christ that even the most frazzled grocery run cannot dim.

When you lie down: I've spoken often of our streamlined approach to bedtime routines. As a homeschooling family who spends hours together talking, reading, working, and playing each day, we eschew drawn-out bedtime stories or evening bath-time rituals in favor of potty, water, teeth, hugs, and kisses (never fear—when my children are truly dirty, we bathe before bed too). But we do leave space for the inevitably chatty child whose greatest life questions always bubble to the surface right before his eyes flutter shut in exhaustion. Our eighth-born, Shiloh, is notorious for whipping out questions like "Does God have legs?" right at bedtime.

Our older children, likewise, linger as bedtime approaches, watching silly videos with us, engaging in theological debates about situational ethics versus pragmatism (yes, actually), and confiding struggles or joys to us.

And I would be remiss if I skipped over those infant nighttime feedings during which, though unable to expound deep truths to our tiny ones as we fill their bellies, we can pray for them or others and preach, without words, the care of their heavenly Father in our devotion to them.

When you get up: If you, like me, have awakened to wailing coming from one of your small children's rooms two hours before your alarm is set to go off, then you know the process of "getting up" can be one of the most sanctifying experiences in parenting. Mornings are often strewn with the land mines of too-early risers, cranky toddlers, teens who ignore their alarms and are late for work, and a mad rush to get out the door for jobs or school.

We have the opportunity as we rise to declare God's grace sufficient for forgotten lunches and missed carpools, sleep deprivation and burnt breakfast.

Clearly, the parental mandate found in these verses requires, if not constant vigilance, at least a willingness to view each aspect of our days as an occasion for godly instruction (for our children), growth (for us and them), and worship.

A Missed Opportunity

One night, as I herded my five youngest to the car after grocery shopping plus dinner and playground time at an impressively multitasking local market, I noticed a family of four "having dinner together" on the patio. The mom caught my eye first. Her head remained bent over her phone, earbuds firmly embedded in both ears, as she ignored her husband and two preteen sons. My brain registered surprise, which blossomed into full-fledged chagrin as I realized the other members of her family were also glued to devices, each just as oblivious as the next.

I can already imagine the indignant emails I'll receive for even describing this scenario:

"You have no idea what that woman dealt with that day. Maybe she'd been with her kids all day long, and this was her first chance for a break."

"You have no business climbing up on a judgmental high horse when you don't live her life or have her children."

Both are true, which is why I'll say that, with zero desire to shame either parent, I felt two emotions upon witnessing this scene:

1. **Sadness**. That tech-heavy dinner was a missed opportunity for the kind of connection that can't be recharged with an iPad plug. Maybe it was an anomaly, a mere blip in a series of screen-free meals I'll never witness. Or maybe it reflects something I can certainly encounter in my own heart—a desire to be "left alone" when I know I should engage.

2. **Conviction**. While our family doesn't typically do screens during dinner, I know myself to be perfectly capable of mentally checking out or avoiding an opportunity for investment when I'm tired or tapped out.

Whether it's establishing house rules for technology at mealtimes, being intentional to ask our children open-ended questions (and actually listen to their answers), choosing to play basketball in the driveway when we really just want to collapse on the couch, or saying yes to "help" with dinner when we'd rather get it done as quickly as possible, mundane, daily life is rife with chances to "impress" upon our children God's goodness and His commandments (which, as we've already pointed out, include "loving our neighbor as ourselves"), if only we can recognize the gift of time and humdrum intentionality.

The true value of a "sit, walk, lie down, and get up" approach to parenting lies in its steadiness. There is no unachievable mandate to wring the last drop of theological import out of every interaction with our children; we are granted a grace-filled perspective that allows us to bounce back from the realization we have been lax in our calling to teach God's truth to our children by simply doing the next thing.

The Pitfalls of Avoidance Parenting

One morning, as I was reading my Bible, a verse I had never noticed before from 1 Kings arrested my attention. It says, "His father had never rebuked him by asking, 'Why do you behave as you do?' He was also very handsome and was born next after Absalom" (1 Kings 1:6 NIV). The English Standard Version of this text puts it this way: "His father had never at any time displeased him by asking, 'Why have you done thus and so?'"

For context, the young man in question here is named Adonijah, and the father is King David.

For such a relatively short verse, it packs a wallop of conviction, so let's break it down.

We're going to skip to the end and talk about Absalom first. In case you're not familiar, Absalom was the most handsome, the most charismatic, and the most rebellious of David's sons. Over the course of multiple chapters in 2 Samuel (with a particular emphasis in chapters 13–19), we learn of Absalom's vengeful nature (he plans and carries out murderous revenge on a half brother who

Mundane LIFE IS RIFE WITH chances TO impress UPON OUR KIDS God's goodness AND His character.

raped Absalom's sister), his cunning (he steals the loyalty of his father's subjects by stroking their egos and passing out promises of a better rule if he were king), his immorality (he sleeps with his father's concubines in broad daylight), and his unchecked ambition (he plans a full-scale coup, which is foiled by a man named Hushai, who remains secretly loyal to David).

Ultimately, none of these can save him from a violent death at the hands of David's soldiers—a demise over which David mourns so publicly that Joab, the commander of his armies, is forced to give the king a stiff pep talk about his duties to his people (whom Absalom manipulated and led astray).

With this background in mind, the fact that his younger brother Adonijah is described as "also very handsome" and "born right after Absalom" feels like some serious foreshadowing. Though there's nothing wrong with being attractive, it's the rare specimen who doesn't feel at least a temptation to use his or her beauty for personal gain. Adonijah's birth order and personal appearance should have prompted some soul-searching in David, who'd already witnessed the devastating repercussions of parental abdication.

Instead of a renewed commitment to being "all in" with his children, though, we see David's repeating past mistakes by choosing the always foolish "avoidance parenting" route.

Raise your hand if you've ever ducked addressing a topic with one of your children because you know their response won't be pretty. We both know I can't actually see your hand in the air right now, but we also both know, if our hands aren't up (mine too!), they probably should be for the sake of honesty. It's not like we can't relate to David's cowardice for the sake of "keeping the peace," but given the ugly chaos that reigned as a result of his choices, we can all agree it was a short-lived lull in what eventually became a storm so epic that it came back for a second squall, courtesy of Adonijah.

Yep, that's right. The younger brother of the anarchist took a page out of Absalom's book and attempted to overthrow his brother Solomon, whom God had appointed as the rightful heir to David's throne. And no one with any knowledge of the situation should have been the least bit surprised.

Intentionality Always Trumps Passivity

I'm always amazed at the richness of God's Word, astonished (though I shouldn't be) so many powerful truths can be layered into a verse I've read at least a dozen times before and never noticed until the Lord opens my eyes to truly see it.

Which brings us right back to that part about doing the next thing. If you don't know what that is, exactly, may I remind you of this: Righteous intentionality trumps limp passivity every single time.

Righteous intentionality trumps limp passivity every single time.

Getting down on eye level with our toddler and calmly addressing the same tantrum she's been throwing at bedtime for five days straight instead of ignoring it in hopes it will fizzle out on its own is a small way to *impress* God's ways on our children.

Making muffins with our nine-year-old on a Saturday morning, then taking the time to ensure she follows through on cleanup, even though it would be easier in the short-term to do it ourselves and avoid the eye rolls and dragged feet, is a small way to *impress* God's ways on our children.

Checking our teen's internet browser history, just like we've said we will, instead of skipping it because we'd rather not find (and address) that questionable website he visited is a small way to *impress* God's ways on our children.

Each "yes" of engagement lays yet another brick of faithfulness, "for no one can lay a foundation other than that which is laid, which is Jesus Christ" (1 Corinthians 3:11).

Full disclosure, friends: The Lord often whispers, "Do you really mean it?" when I share convictions He has taught me from His Word. Am I truly preaching to myself just as much as to my mama friends?

The answer is yes.

I wrote most of these words on an eight-hour ride home from a speaking gig at a homeschool conference with the whole family in tow—a ride that included many quiet moments of napping, audiobooks, and game playing but that was also peppered with whining and demands from grumpy toddlers, many iterations of "Are we there yet?" and "I'm *hungry*," and a bit of huffing over whose turn it was to use the tablet to watch a movie.

Many of these commonplace kerfuffles occurred while I typed the sentences you've just read. And wouldn't you know it? Just as we were unloading the car upon our arrival home, and I got to the part about the need to press in when it would be easier to tap out, one of my twin toddlers walked by babbling about the potty, covered in very obvious proof that the window for "potty time" had passed.

Part of me wanted to let Shaun deal with it—to keep my train of thought while someone else picked up my slack. But the irony of encouraging others in steadfastness while dodging an unpleasant task crashed through my concentration, and I snagged the fragrant little rascal and hauled him off to the bathtub instead.

If you sometimes don't *want* to do right, me too. If you *don't* do right all the time as a result of your sinful desires, me too. But if you also sometimes do right anyway because the Holy Spirit won't leave you alone, and you desire to honor and glorify Him, even in seemingly silly acts of obedience, me too! And if you often need motivation to keep doing the third, in spite of the first two, read on, sister!

Because we are called to more than merely avoiding a vague end-of-life regret at not having "spent more time with our kids."

We are called to a life of conscious, caring commitment to God first and then our closest neighbors as we "sit, walk, lie down, and get up." And the good news is the Lord is sitting, walking, lying down, and getting up with us every step of the way.

A Titus Two Perspective

SALLY CLARKSON

writer, podcast host, conference speaker, mother of four

One midnight, when I was exhausted to my toenails, my little three-year-old Joy climbed into my bed and squished her little body as close to mine as she could get. "Mama, I feel best when I am close to you. Then I can be happy and fall asleep."

We imagine that to do great things in the world, we need to accomplish important work. However, kingdom work is about not just moving to the most impoverished country or preaching to thousands but also laying down our lives right where we are in the hidden moments of life, loving the one right in front of us. When a child longs to have our comforting touch and gentle voice speaking life-giving words, he may remember and be able to imagine the voice and touch of God when he ponders faith as a young adult and may choose to believe because the reality of God was tangible in his home.

The child who needs one more song to be comforted before sleeping will, in adulthood, believe in a God who is patient and willing to answer prayer and hear our voice when we, as His children, cry out in faith.

The child who is lonely, confused, and hormonal will feel the touch of God, the sacrifice of God, because we gave up the rights to our time and comfort to befriend, listen, and show compassion and sympathy for what is on his heart.

Love is given through a candle lit and a special breakfast served on Sunday before church as we open the Gospel together, demonstrating that the reality and beauty of God's creativity is validated in how we live. It is shown with the sacrificial life of giving up what we wanted to do, or the job we hoped to have, to build a soul by giving a child our attention—looking into the child's eyes with true interest and compassion instead of looking at a screen while half-heartedly listening. These are the sacrifices of our love, the moment-by-moment giving up of ourselves, the constant, year-in-year-out practice of worship as we serve those in our home in order to please His heart.

It is for Him, for His kingdom, that we serve with willing, generous, life-giving hearts, as the building of His kingdom is one heart at a time.

The Narrative

A WORLDLY RESPONSE TO "WORTH IT"	A BIBLICAL RESPONSE TO "WORTH IT"
Looks for ways to escape the pinch of daily child-rearing responsibilities	Leans into the repetitive rhythms of motherhood as a means of grace-filled parenting over perfection
Resents being needed so much	Rejoices in the vital nature of her role
Passes the buck when parenting red flags emerge	Notices problematic behavior and prayerfully addresses it

Action Steps

- Memorize and meditate on Deuteronomy 6:6-7 (NIV): "These commandments that I give you today are to be on your hearts. Impress them on your children. Talk about them when you sit at home and when you walk along the road, when you lie down and when you get up."
- If you're able, have a conversation with your spouse about boundaries for technology use in your home. Use the guidelines: when, for how long, at what age, and with what frequency?
- Write down one intentional activity you can do with your children in each of the "sit, walk, lie down, get up" categories this week. Put at least two of them into practice.

Questions

What are two areas in which you are intentional to disciple your children?

What are two areas in which you are lax about intentional discipleship?

Why is it often easier to avoid addressing our children's problematic behavior? Is this approach biblical? Why or why not?

Prayer

Father, You demonstrate throughout Your Word that You love us too much to simply leave us to our own desires. May we learn from Your perfect example as we strive to consistently and intentionally convey Your goodness to our children each and every day. Amen.

CHAPTER 3

Perseverance, Patience, and Praise

Our family's first stop on our six-week trip to Europe was Paris. We booked an apartment in the fifth arrondissement, a short walk from Luxembourg Gardens. The photos from the online listing were atypical. Instead of uncluttered surfaces and clean, staged living rooms, this rental boasted colorful, haphazard bookshelves stuffed with knickknacks and novels, rumpled bedding, and a postage-stamp-sized kitchen with nary a square inch of available counter space. Still, the price was right, and the reviews were stellar, with hundreds of guests raving about the location, cheerful style, warm hosts, and access to everything needed.

We communicated our unusually large party size and age range to the host, and she answered favorably and enthusiastically. And so it was that, as all thirteen of us trooped up four flights of winding stairs to reach the apartment, I felt excitement simmering underneath my bedraggled exhaustion from two full days of travel.

But as we shimmied our way through the narrow door into an even more cramped hallway, my heart sank. The photos hadn't been a bid for relatability. They were accurate. This space was the very definition of "lived in," with the host's belongings in plain view on multiple surfaces at a glance. For a family with older kids, this might have been a nuisance at worst. But for a family with so many small children, this rental was a recipe for chaos.

Each day was a fight to keep our things from getting mixed in with the host family's possessions (our oldest son mysteriously misplaced two new pairs of jeans and a pair of AirPods the second day, and we never found them), and the sleeping arrangements were labyrinthine, with multiple pull-down ladders, closet-sized bedrooms, and narrow lofts pieced together to provide enough beds for us all (our children—who have slept on floors and couches aplenty—still talk about sitting up too quickly in sleepy forgetfulness each morning and bashing their heads into the ceiling).

Still, we were in *Paris*, and this rental—which we chose!—was nothing if not an adventure.

If your mind snagged a bit on the part where I mentioned thirteen of us, let me explain: Yes, we have ten children, which should bring our family total to twelve, but we hired the adult daughter of a family friend to help count heads when we were out and about and also to stay with younger children during naptimes or in the evening if Shaun and I were out with older kids.

A Lesson on Toddlers and Cupboards

During one such occasion, Shaun got home from playing basketball with the older boys in Luxembourg Gardens first (the girls and I were still out sightseeing) and discovered a scene of utter mayhem.

The twinbies had woken early from their naps in the room they shared with us and proceeded to stealthily disembowel every single drawer and cupboard in a built-in cabinet along one wall. Our friend's daughter had heard brief rustlings she took to be their waking movements but nothing to indicate the level of havoc they'd wreaked.

To our utter horror, we discovered the rental's owner had left folders full of important personal documents inside these cabinets, unlocked and readily accessible to even the nosiest and least considerate of guests (see: two-year-olds).

The drawers were also full of office supplies, and I distinctly recall striding through the kitchen upon arriving home to the spectacle of Shaun and Ezra on their knees, attempting to restore order to the mountain of papers on the floor, and feeling something sharp embed itself into the very depths of my heel pad. I'd love to tell you my response was cool and collected, but the truth is I *shrieked*, "A TACK! There is a TACK in my foot!" before hobbling to sit on the bed in the trashed room and yank it out.

Friends.

If ever there were a moment when this trip seemed like a bad idea, this was it.

A mere three days into the "adventure," the prospect of multiple weeks of untold repeat debacles loomed large as we sifted through bank statements, lien agreements, and passport documents. (If you just gasped, same.)

The urge to bail was strong. Perhaps this entire trip had been a miscalculation. After all, we'd done our best to plan ahead to have ample help, and still, every effort had been smoothly foiled by the slyness of two tiny humans who regularly put their pants on backward and inside out.

A Bad Time to Make Big Decisions

One tidbit of wisdom passed down to me from multiple mentors, which I am likewise generous to sprinkle into the lives of others, is this: Never make big or permanent decisions in moments of duress.

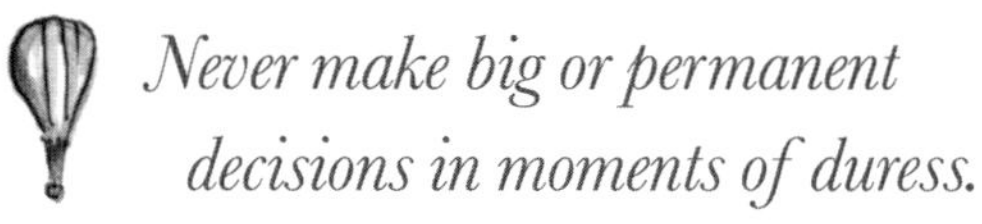

Never make big or permanent decisions in moments of duress.

The most obvious example I've encountered is family size. I've lost count of the number of sorrowful messages I've received from parents who chose to irrevocably alter their bodies to keep from having more kids.

"If only we'd waited a few more months," they sigh.

Until the colic died down. Until the seemingly impossible job situation resolved itself. Until the overwhelm of twins faded a bit.

Can I guarantee that a challenging situation will always resolve itself favorably or that we won't transition from one exhausting season directly into another? You know I can't. And yet the Bible has way more to say about the value of perseverance for believers than it does about guaranteed "rainbows and sparkles" outcomes this side of heaven.

The Bible has way more to say about the value of perseverance for believers than it does about guaranteed "rainbows and sparkles" outcomes this side of heaven.

Here are just a few gems about exercising spiritual grit:

- "For you have need of endurance, so that when you have done the will of God you may receive what is promised" (Hebrews 10:36).
- "Blessed is a man who perseveres under trial; for once he has been approved, he will receive the crown of life which the Lord has promised to those who love Him" (James 1:12 NASB).
- "Make every effort to add to your faith goodness; and to goodness, knowledge; and to knowledge, self-control; and to self-control, ***perseverance***; and to ***perseverance***, godliness...For if you possess these qualities...they will keep you from being ineffective and unproductive in your knowledge of our Lord Jesus Christ" (2 Peter 1:5-8 NIV, emphasis mine).

- “We rejoice in our sufferings, knowing that suffering produces endurance, and endurance produces character, and character produces hope” (Romans 5:3-4).

That last passage gut punches me every time as I contemplate how often I’ve essentially asked God to either “fix the problem” or, if not, place an IV line of patience or steadfastness or joy into my veins. Yet all the while, He’s placing me in situations that, through His Holy Spirit’s transformation of my character in the midst of them, produce the true hope of a changed heart rather than the temporary relief of an eased circumstance.

Through, Not Around

Spoiler alert: We did not, in fact, pack up our belongings (the ones we could find anyway), vacate the premises of that problematic rental in disgrace, and herd our entire crew onto the first flight home to Texas.

Instead, we told our host the whole truth and nothing but the truth, complete with pictorial evidence of the damage. And you know what? She took it in stride. She was gracious and understanding. And I think we both came away with some important lessons learned about toddlers and cupboards.

I’d love to say this was the only sticky situation traveling with twin toddlers got us into on that trip, but I’d be lying. (Don’t worry; I’ll share more later.)

Still, I’m so glad we didn’t cave to the temptation either to abandon ship or to proceed with a clenched jaw of dread for the future. Because neither deserting our post nor squinting at it with continual distrust serves us well on the battlefield of parenting (after that anecdote, I doubt anyone needs an explanation for the military terms currently coming to mind for this whole parenting gig).

Maybe you’re a mom of young children whose husband is deployed, and you’re burned out.

Maybe you’re a new homeschool mom having a rough first year.

Maybe you’re a full-time working mom drowning in deadlines and diapers.

Maybe you’re a mom of a child failing constantly at controlling his urges toward destruction and defiance.

What if the answer is not endless screen time (for them or you), barely holding on until wine o'clock, or signing your kids up for anything and everything that keeps them out of the house?

What if, instead of trying to escape, we embraced engagement for the purpose of long-lasting solutions?

At the homeschool conference I referenced earlier, a young mom of three approached, eager to share twin shenanigans with someone she knew would relate.

After several anecdotes during which I chuckled and nodded along with something that was, at times, more cringing recognition than fondness, she mentioned her twin daughters' propensity for staying up much too late. One, in particular, was so wired and destructive her mom found herself grasping at any possible relief.

While medication was the most obvious work-around, it was her own mother's seemingly "out there" suggestion (which she gleaned from an online article) to cut back on foods laced with dyes that caught this mama's attention. "I'm *so* not a natural or crunchy mom," she told me. "But if there was a chance it could help, I figured it wouldn't hurt to try."

To her amazement, the experiment not only "worked" but produced a transformed child almost immediately. Instead of quite literally bouncing off the walls until 11:00 p.m. every night, her newly dye-free daughter listened to instructions and fell asleep at a reasonable hour.

"She's still an active toddler, don't get me wrong," said the mom. "But it's no longer the kind of energy that stretches me to breaking."

I felt myself breathing a sigh of relief for her, months after the behavior had already improved. I've never encountered this exact scenario with my own children, but I certainly can relate to the intense relief of a crisis resolved.

Friends, this is what moving *through* adversity (instead of trying to find a way around it) looks like. This grateful mama told me it took real grit for a season to resist her daughters' requests for the treats they'd received in the past and to research which foods to avoid, but she acknowledged the effort was *worth it*. "Plus," she said with a smile, "we don't eat nearly as much junk anymore, and that's a good thing too, I guess."

Band-Aids Are Not Cures

Since the theme of the moment is twins, I'll share with you another anecdote that still makes my nose wrinkle in disgust at the memory of it.

When our twin boys were three and a half, they suddenly became quite artistic.

Lest you be too impressed, I feel compelled to share that their favorite medium was—*drumroll, please*—poop.

They had all but given up their afternoon naps but would still happily trundle off to their nursery to play together each afternoon, which was a welcome break from the constant stream of cute-but-destructively-busy activity that defined their existence at the time. If you've read *Hard Is Not the Same Thing as Bad*, then you know our twin girls took us on a merrily tempestuous ride through the wilds of toddlerhood—a ride that left us reeling and gasping for breath, even as seasoned toddler parents of three older children.

Titus and Toby's three-year-old antics (sometimes) involved less screaming in the car but were equally as energetic and far more ferocious. With their golden halos of curls, twinkly blue eyes, and delicate, heart-shaped faces, they bring to mind Raphaelite images of charming cherubs. But it takes only one episode of witnessing their propensity for "attackling" each other (find me a more apt word for toddler takedowns—I'll wait) or one instance of walking through the closet that separates our bedroom from their room and colliding with a wall of stench emanating from their *closed* nursery door to realize that angelic they are not.

Everything in me wants to tell you this pooptastrophe (we're talking walls, floors, windows, crib bars, bedding, stuffed animals, the *works*) was the only one. But it wasn't. I remember sharing about this phase on social media and having a reader confidently assert that, if only I would have them help clean up the mess, the problem would disappear. That's what she had done with her own child, and it would work for me too.

It's not a bad suggestion. And it is an example of working *through*, rather than around, the issue. But I couldn't help but chuckle because, despite helping scrub mattresses and floors, our little Poopcassos possessed artists' souls too pure to give up their craft.

I once heard someone say, "One little boy, one brain. Two little boys, half a brain. Three or more little boys, no brains at all." As a mama to five stair-step boys, ages ten and under, I knew exactly what she meant. My girls, who are all grouped in age, can get punch-drunk when goofing off together, but the level of little boy "wolf pack" groupthink that turns our living room into a war zone of scattered throw pillows and tipped-over side tables each night is truly a cacophonous wonder to behold.

Throw in the twin factor of two little boys at the exact same developmental stage, and you have both zero brains (because they *knew* it was wrong, but they could not seem to think ahead to the inevitable consequences of their smelly life choices) and the most deviously aligned brains possible (based on the scenes we found, they both agreed that touching the poop with their own hands or bodies was *disgusting*—duh—and they would work in concert to use clothing, diapers, toys, sheets, and even book pages, to do their, *ahem*, dirty work).

If you're wondering why we didn't separate them immediately, in hindsight, so am I a bit. Sometimes, when you're in "it" (if you get my drift), it takes some time to figure out how to climb out.

We tried everything we could think of before we resorted to the separation option—removing all potential "paintbrushes" but the most essential bedding and clothing, requiring them to join the cleanup crew, giving various consequences, pep talking them into "clean thoughts" before naptime. It didn't feel like lobbing bombs of desperation but instead working through the obvious answers at hand in hopes of a workable solution. Plus, there was one huge deterrent from putting them in separate rooms: We didn't have a great place to put just one little mess-making boy that didn't involve introducing him to his older brother's room (and all its wondrous toys, books, and other potential implements for spreading fecal matter across the walls).

We'd also been putting off potty training, despite the twinbies already being the longest to wear diapers. We'd just moved back into our home after a six-month stint in a rental, and on top of homeschooling, unpacking and recombobulating our house after a forced remodel (more on that later), travel for work (for Shaun and me), speaking events, and soccer (plus other activities) for the kids, consistency in potty training was nonexistent.

But after one particularly stomach-turning cleanup session that took multiple family members over an hour (and two loads of laundry) to set to right, Shaun and I agreed we could no longer hope for the best (a hope the twinbies would nurse by going long stretches without practicing their art, only to dive back in with gusto just when they had lulled us into complacency).

Turns out, despite our best efforts to work through the muck, we'd been slapping Paw Patrol Band-Aids on a gaping wound, and it was time to stitch it up and let it heal.

So we took the plunge and put one little twinbie in Shiloh's room, officially emancipating his older brother from a naptime that had been spotty at best for a while.

It was heart-wrenching to listen to Titus's wails for "my Toby" as I made the judgment call to keep him in the nursery, gambling that he'd been the primary instigator. But you know what? My mama's heart healed almost instantaneously when (praise be!) they both settled down after about twenty minutes, and (miracle of miracles) fell asleep for two blessed hours.

And then they did the same thing day after day.

All my hesitations about separation—robbing them of their playtime, introducing another environment to trash, losing my break from twintastrophes outside of the nursery—dissolved in one painfully blissful moment of ripping that Band-Aid of what-ifs right off.

The momentum from this choice propelled us to begin potty training in earnest, and, while the rewards weren't nearly as immediate, I'm happy to report that our now five-year-old twin boys do not, in fact, still wear diapers.

When We Already Know the Answer...

I share all this to remind you that "worth it" rarely presents itself in a quick fix (although glory hallelujah when it does!).

PERSEVERANCE, PATIENCE,
AND PRAISE. . .
ARE FOUNDATIONAL
TO BIBLICAL
PARENTING.

I share all this to remind you that "worth it" rarely presents itself in a quick fix (although glory hallelujah when it does!).

Yes, there are many bad habits we can curb with short bursts of concentrated effort (I talk about this in more depth in my "Boot Camp Parenting" chapter of *M Is for Mama*). But more often than not, the efforts that make this whole motherhood thing worthwhile and effect true change in both ourselves and our children require a "long obedience in the same direction" (to quote one of the few things Friedrich Nietzsche and I agree on). This is true no matter your stage in life and no matter your number of children.

Even seasoned mamas of many find themselves scrambling to pivot, regroup, and rethink solutions to challenging scenarios. I have always striven to remind you the goal is growth, not perfection, and that there is no prescription for "success" in parenting beyond merely refusing to give in or give up as we seek to honor God in everything we do—including using a plastic scraper to remove poop from windowsills.

I'll leave you with this bit of encouragement. If you read the intro to *Hard Is Not the Same Thing as Bad* and remember my despair at Nola's car rage, my questioning of the Lord's purpose in squashing my pride and testing my patience again and again, then hear this: I'm not the same mama I was then, because the Lord is so kind not to leave us where He finds us.

And I can prove it.

One afternoon, upon discovering another fragrant fiasco in the nursery after feeling we'd finally made a breakthrough with the twinbies, I felt hot tears of resentment welling in my eyes. I'm not naturally prone to crying, and I honestly hadn't felt anything even akin to despair with the previous episodes, despite my exasperation. But this time—on a day filled to the brim with "more important stuff"—felt like a mocking blow to my ability to get anything done with either promptness or dignity.

As I scrubbed, I found the sentence "Why, God..." forming in my brain. Hear me, friends. The Lord can handle our questioning. But He had already responded to this query of mine more than once. And I knew the answer. (The short version is "for my good and for His glory.") So instead of finishing the rant, I began to sing a medley of worship songs that has become my go-to when "rejoicing always" (Philippians 4:4) feels just beyond the stretch of my fingertips.

These three songs ("I Love You, Lord," "More Precious than Silver," and "I Exalt Thee") have kept me company through sleepless nights, puking episodes, repugnant chores, and solo-parenting stints. They are not pure Scripture, but they are paraphrased verses, solidly rooted in biblical truth, and have the same powerful potential for peace of mind and spirit.

As I scraped and sang, my angst melted away. It didn't change the fact that I had missed out on a writing session (for this very book) I'd been looking forward to and that I was now behind on dinner prep. But it did change my outlook, which was more important in that moment.

Sometimes we don't have an answer that will immediately soothe away all our woes. Sometimes we glimpse God's bigger purpose in the hardships we face but feel nervous we're wrong (or the path will be hard). Yet through His kindness to plunge us into difficulty yet again, we eventually come to realize that, while the particular strategies may vary, the principles—perseverance, patience, and praise—are timeless, unchanging, and foundational to biblical parenting.

A Titus Two Perspective

JENNIFER PEPITO

author, podcast host, mother of seven

Missions were always part of our family vision. When I was pregnant with my first of seven children, we attended missionary conferences, and we began pursuing missions in China when our second was a baby. We quickly changed gears as we discovered that this mission organization required you to have fewer than four children to be part of their group. We were excited to expand our family and didn't want to wait, but we didn't want to give up on our family vision either. As I added more children to our family, we continued reading missionary biographies, supporting missionaries, and learning about the wide world until, finally, an opportunity came for us when we had five young children to take over a mission to migrant workers south of the border.

Amid concerns from our extended family, we packed up our five kids in a green Chevy Astro van and drove across the border into Mexico. During the four years there, we hosted family groups, helped an orphanage, welcomed another baby, and discipled families. We also dealt with chicken pox and seizures, bleeding from a routine tonsillectomy, and an emergency C-section after an episode of maternal bleeding. There was a lot of blood, sweat, and tears in those four years as missionaries, and by the time we left, we were ragged and worn, our family vision a little frail around the edges.

I write more about this season in *Mothering by the Book*, but regaining our family vision after such an intense four years of ministry wasn't easy. We had faced many challenges as missionaries, and the fallout from that season wasn't over in a moment. It wasn't until we learned some spiritual warfare skills that we began to find our equilibrium again so that hope and purpose could be restored.

Spiritual Warfare Skills

When you go through a hardship, it can be tempting to try to escape it, or even make the hardship worse by reacting to it. This can cause the pain from the experience to multiply as we heap bad decisions atop the normal hardships of life.

This is what we learned to do:

> **Forgive.** God has forgiven us and asks us to forgive others quickly so we don't give the enemy a foothold (see Ephesians 4:26-27). Instead of holding on to offense, quietly release it to God while letting Him comfort you for the pain you've experienced. This act of forgiveness was not just a step but a leap toward regaining our family vision. It was integral to our journey of healing and restoration.
>
> **Give thanks.** As I learned to appreciate the goodness in my life and let go of bitterness, hope grew. It wasn't that circumstances instantly got better but rather that I learned to give thanks even while it was hard. This practice of thankfulness was a transformative tool that helped us see the light in the midst of darkness.
>
> **Sing.** Singing activates calming hormones and puts a stop to meditating on what is hard in our lives. I sing hymns, worship songs, psalms, or even silly songs to move my thoughts out of negative ruts and into hope.

As we began to heal from the hardships of our original missionary adventure, new doors opened to us. We took all seven of our children to Tanzania, Africa, to lead a marriage conference for missionaries; we went to Assisi, Italy, to experience the places where St. Francis lived; and many of my children have gone on to take their own mission trips. We still have hardships on these trips, but because we have tools for spiritual warfare, we are able to stay in forgiveness, cultivate thankfulness, and just keep singing.

The Narrative

A WORLDLY RESPONSE TO "WORTH IT"	A BIBLICAL RESPONSE TO "WORTH IT"
Wants to throw in the towel as soon as things get tough	Knows that perseverance through inevitable rough patches pays off
Ignores the effect negativity has on her perspective	Acknowledges the power of "rejoicing in all things," even when "enjoying all things" is impossible
Looks for ways to circumvent challenges at all costs	Commits to finding a way *through* difficulty to peace on the other side

Action Steps

- Memorize and meditate on 2 Peter 1:5-8 (NIV): "Make every effort to add to your faith goodness; and to goodness, knowledge; and to knowledge, self-control; and to self-control, perseverance; and to perseverance, godliness...For if you possess these qualities...they will keep you from being ineffective and unproductive in your knowledge of our Lord Jesus Christ."
- Identify a time in motherhood in which you felt stuck or ready to throw in the towel. Write down at least three things that made you feel that way.
- Write down one lesson the Lord taught you in the midst of that hard time.

Questions

Has there ever been a time you were tempted to make a permanent decision based on a temporary difficulty? How did that go?

What is one biblical truth you can preach to yourself when your current circumstances feel overwhelming or as if they will never change?

What is one practical step you can take to move through a difficult stage, rather than simply try to go around it?

Prayer

Father, thank You that no matter how many messes we make, You remain faithful to provide a way through. Grant us eyes to see Your sovereign hand in even the most frustrating circumstances and trust that You are using difficult situations in our lives for our good and for Your glory. Amen.

CHAPTER 4

It's Not Destruction, It's Development

Similar to the uptick in chatter about "child-free living," a rising trend on social media is to talk about the "complexity" or "nuance" surrounding the "question of whether to have children." In a random scroll through the "explore" page on Instagram one evening (which is 90 percent nonsense, 5 percent creative and ingenious content, and 5 percent nonsense that is nevertheless useful to keeping a finger on the pulse of culture), I stumbled upon a young mother responding to a video of a Gen Z woman fluttering her hands and grimacing uncomfortably with a caption meant to explain her contortions: "Women having complex feelings about having children because it can destroy their body, career, and mental health."

Lest anyone assume this is a fringe perspective, the post had 745,000 likes and almost 20,000 comments (most of them agreeing with the poster and elaborating with aggressive and hostile descriptions of the horrors of having children).

The young mother responding to this video proceeded to give a strongly worded clapback—affirming the value of motherhood and expositing the pitfalls of a society that considers a body changed by pregnancy and striped with stretch marks (hello, book title) to be "destroyed."

While I applauded her fervor, I couldn't help but cringe in anticipation as I opened the comment section.

Sure enough, in response to her impassioned defense of motherhood came a deluge of "nobody cares about stretch marks; having kids is downright dangerous; you've missed the point; have some nuance." The first comment I encountered (which was split in two to allow the commenter to include every last word) contained paragraphs of possible pregnancy- and birth-related complications (clearly copied and pasted from an internet search)—many of them extremely rare and some downright bizarre—and ended with a mocking "But sure, we're just worried about our figures" and a yawning emoji.

I think Thomas Carlyle was onto something when he said (in reference to his own propensity for it), "Sarcasm I now see to be, in general, the language of the devil."[1]

Setting aside the fact that "internet people" are not known for their ability to carry on a civil disagreement when a screen separates them from the bearer of God's image with whom they contend, I couldn't help but acknowledge the validity of at least one aspect of the commenter's point.

Marked by Motherhood

As a result of Adam and Eve's sin and rebellion against God, the curse of the fall entered this world. For women, this carries a unique consequence: "[God] will surely multiply your pain in childbearing; in pain you shall bring forth children" (Genesis 3:16).

The Bible doesn't deny that pregnancy and childbirth are painful and difficult, but this is a far cry from a claim that this pain and difficulty then "destroy" us. In fact, Jesus goes on to say this: "When a woman is giving birth, she has sorrow because her hour has come, but when she has delivered the baby, she no longer remembers the anguish, for the joy that a human being has been born into the world" (John 16:21).

As a woman who has given birth ten times, experienced seven unmedicated labors (and one epidural, which wore off in my lower half about an hour before delivering my second set of twins), I can affirm Jesus's words to be 100 percent accurate. Several of my labors lasted for well over twenty-four hours (my first was forty-four hours of contractions that, while not as intense in the beginning as they were during transition, never stopped and kept me awake for two full nights). The last two hours of my seventh child's birth were a blur of back labor and mentally begging, "Lord, please take this one for me. I can't do this anymore."

And you know what? He did. I survived. And the moment all nine pounds, one ounce of our sweet Honor Daniel were out in the air-breathing world, I experienced immediate relief from the agony I thought might snap my back in two.

And you know what else? It was worth it! I would say I'd do it all again to have him, but the fact I went on to have three more children makes that a little obvious.

Now, for those of you thinking, "That's nice, Abbie. But my issues didn't end with delivery. Having children wrought permanent changes in my body and mind, and they weren't all for the better," I get it.

I did six months of pelvic floor therapy after the twinbies were born (happy to say I reduced my prolapse to an asymptomatic grade 2 case, which allows me to exercise, lift my children, and do any other physical activity I desire, provided I pay attention to my symptoms, watch my form, and choose wisely).

I have gnarly varicose veins that snake down my right leg and can flare up painfully during my cycle each month (amazingly, they did not worsen during my last twin pregnancy and now bother me less—both physically and mentally—than they used to).

One of my ribs is forever bent from being donkey kicked for the last three months of my second pregnancy.

My sacrum is twisted from delivering my nine-pound, two ounce, 23.5-inch second born (he really did a number!), which means, unless I've just seen the chiropractor, one of my legs is almost an inch shorter than the other (it's always tricky to arrange my pant legs just right so as to not appear lopsided).

I have a flat chest from breastfeeding ten babies, a not-as-flat-as-before midsection from carrying them, stretch marks across my hips, a funky belly button, and odd little wrinkles on the inside of my left forearm that I finally realized were the result of carrying so many babies and toddlers on that hip for so many years (check the inside of your arm right above your wrist; you might have them too!).

I've experienced relatively easy pregnancies and more-or-less-straightforward deliveries. (Though there was a moment when, after presenting transverse, then being roughly flipped and pulled limb by limb from my womb, Toby—a.k.a. twinbie number two—came out gray and floppy, and I was frantic with worry. Praise God, he was good to go after an hour of oxygen.) But I know what it's like to manually lift my elephantine legs, grotesque with twin pregnancy edema, into bed filled with despair that my balloon toes will ever deflate. I have experienced the agony of pubic symphysis pain as my hips separated to allow for two babies to have enough room at the end of pregnancy. I know too well the gasp-inducing fire of tweaked double round ligaments when I sit up from teaching the chest press track in my fitness classes (side note: I didn't know the kind of pain I was capable of hiding until I faced a roomful of people who would surely have rushed to my side if my expression reflected my torment).

It was only in retrospect that I recognized the mild postpartum depression I experienced after having my first set of twins (it went away on its own in about six months as my hormones regulated). Then, I battled postpartum anxiety for over a year after our seventh child's birth (exacerbated by our move into a very in-progress house we were building ourselves and a difficult friendship breakup I talk about in more detail in *Hard Is Not the Same Thing as Bad*). And the postpartum rage I dealt with after our eighth baby was born ended up being the catalyst for the Gentleness Challenge—a thirty-day commitment to retraining our angry mom brains with Scripture and kind speech.[2]

I don't say any of this to frighten prospective mothers who might be reading this or to dissuade anyone from having children. Quite the opposite. I share to acknowledge the very real toll the incredible privilege of carrying and bringing another human being into this world can have and yet to declare in the same breath that *it is well, well worth it.*

I share to acknowledge the very real toll the incredible privilege of carrying and bringing another human being into this world can have and yet to declare in the same breath that ***it is well, well worth it.***

Afflicted but Not Crushed

Practically everything worth doing—learning a new skill, increasing physical stamina, writing a book, building a house, memorizing a musical piece, taking an epic trip, (fill in your blank)—will require some level of growing pains, some aspect of struggle. How very odd, then, to assume that something so momentous and weighty as birthing children should have no effect on our bodies, minds, and souls.

And how very shortsighted to assume those effects will be universally destructive. After all, so often the things that threaten to break us at first have the power to make us stronger in the end (I'm not one to quote Kelly Clarkson lyrics, but...*she's not wrong*).

In every struggle in pregnancy, birth, and beyond, I experienced the tender mercies of my Savior, who bore my sorrows upon His shoulders when I could not (Isaiah 53:4), kindly nudged me toward repentance through His Holy Spirit when I strayed (Romans 2:4), and provided a "way of escape, that [I might] be able to endure" when I was tempted to succumb to self-pity and resentment (1 Corinthians 10:13).

Again, if you find yourself resisting my insistence of the worthiness of walking through the sometimes fiery landscape of bringing children into this world because I have not listed your particular woe, I can do no more than share my own experience (which will exceed the difficulty of some struggles and pale in comparison to others) and encourage you to consider biblical principles (which are true for all) over any worldly claims of the "destructive" qualities of motherhood.

After all, when Paul describes his endeavors to share Christ, he says this: "We are afflicted in every way, but not crushed; perplexed, but not driven to despair; persecuted, but not forsaken; struck down, but not destroyed" (2 Corinthians 4:8-9).

I don't know about you, but I don't believe any of my children have ever *persecuted* me, despite the internet's insistence that five-year-olds are bullies.

And so we examine the true lack of nuance and complexity in the claim that "having children can destroy your body, career, and mental health."

Because such an assertion not only intentionally paints the prospect of having children in the bleakest shades imaginable, but it simultaneously fails to acknowledge the many ways the gift of children constructs (not tears down) our legacy.

It may be true not every career will flourish with children under our roofs. But is that so bad? We allow many factors to influence the jobs we choose, and most of us do not pursue the same vocation our entire lives. Surely, the mini-mes who spread-eagle drowsy bodies on top of ours and nestle downy heads beneath our chins each morning warrant a hefty say in the "career success" conversation.

It is also true, as I have acknowledged at length, that our mother bodies will change, at least a little (and perhaps very much), as a result of bearing children. But do we truly believe that stretch marks are reserved for mamas or that saggy breasts and dimpled thighs (or any host of non-cosmetic physical ailments) will not eventually beset us with age or accident or gravity?

I have pondered (for a lengthy five seconds) which child I would like to have done without for the sake of five more years of a smaller waist, and here's my conclusion: not one.

The Important Stuff

And what of mental health?

What of wandering into the pantry to wonder why in the name of canned peaches you're there? What of sleepless fogginess, of memory loss and feeling as if you have a bowl of spaghetti noodles, instead of gray matter, in your noggin?

It's true. "Mommy brain" is far from just, *ahem*, in your head. Anyone who has ever found her keys in the fridge knows this. But neither is it all negative. Sure, you may have lost some of the gray matter that helps you remember your second-grade teacher's name, but certain studies suggest becoming a mother actually *increases* the size of a woman's brain in specific areas, "particularly those related to motivation, reward and emotion processing...reasoning and judgment." (This was true exclusively of women who felt warmly toward their newborns and did not struggle with postpartum depression.[3]) In other words, God made our brains able to adapt in order to prioritize the most important stuff while jettisoning much of the flotsam. (Now, if only we could convince said brains that the location of our car keys always falls in the "important stuff" category.)

Not only that, but research indicates moms are often more productive than their childless counterparts[4]—probably because we know we have only forty-three minutes of naptime to swap the laundry, load the dishwasher, finish sewing that last piece of the costume for the Christmas play, and answer at least three emails. I'm certainly not always this productive when I have the chance (sometimes I take a power nap or sit down to eat a snack and scroll my phone), but I do know I've become a much more proficient time manager than before I had kids, if for no other reason than living in chaos is more exhausting than saying I'm too tired to do dishes again.

The benefits of fertility are long-term as well. Studies have shown women who bear three or more children to be 12 percent less likely to develop Alzheimer's—a risk factor that decreases further the more children a woman has.[5]

Conversely, many of the mental struggles we experience following birth don't stick around forever (even though the increased time management and organizational skills often do). I personally know women who dealt with intense (but temporary) periods of postpartum depression. And still, they do not regret their children. One friend even suffered through a strange-sounding syndrome called dysphoric milk ejection reflex, which includes intensely negative thoughts of hopelessness and self-loathing during nursing letdown. It lasts only a few minutes, but considering how often newborns need to eat, it's easy to imagine how this could affect a mama's morale, not to mention her bond with her child.

My friend, a strong, Bible-believing Christian, recognized her struggle as both rare and temporary and chose to pray and quote scriptural truths to herself as she continued to feed her baby. (For those who will object to her perseverance, let me be clear: I do not think it would have been sinful or a "cop-out" had she chosen to bottle-feed, but I love that she found her comfort in God's Word and not merely in the temporary nature of the affliction.)

Far from destroying us, "this light momentary affliction is preparing for us an eternal weight of glory beyond all comparison" (2 Corinthians 4:17). It is up to us to recognize the gift of the "forever" perspective embedded in that passage.

The Intangible Benefits

Even in this earthly realm, childbearing continues to provide us with so many unexpected benefits. Pregnancy and childbirth lower the risk of multiple reproductive cancers, including uterine, ovarian, endometrial, and breast cancers. And breastfeeding adds further protection as the process of pregnancy and lactation makes your breast cells more cancer resistant.[6] Breastfeeding and pregnancy are also linked to lower risks of heart disease and multiple sclerosis (having five or more pregnancies reduces your risk of developing MS by 94 percent; interestingly, the phenomenon of higher numbers of births continuing to lower the risks of disease is consistent across multiple categories).[7]

And then there are the "intangible" benefits: increased joy, elevated purpose, a more selfless worldview, and more, not less, *fun*. As my friends Katie and Elisha Voetberg noted during an interview on my podcast (*M Is for Mama*), "We appreciate doing activities with our kids more than we did before we had them. Skiing is great when you don't have kids. But teaching your child to ski and watching him start to 'get it' is the best. We'll happily go down the bunny slopes to be able to be part of that."[8]

With five small children, this young couple has had plenty of opportunity to test their "level up" attitude—a perspective I find so much more refreshing than a recent social media post that snarked, "I still do all the same things I did before I had kids; they just ruin the experience."

Perspective really is the magic word here. Because the truth is, while I love watching my kids learn new skills, I can also acknowledge that it's both easier and more enjoyable sometimes to exercise those same skills on my own without interruptions of the cute, chubby-cheeked variety.

It doesn't have to be one or the other. Life truly can be sweet before children and even sweeter after—with one of the rewarding aspects being the genuine appreciation we gain for experiences we used to take for granted.

Life truly can be sweet before children and even sweeter after—with one of the rewarding aspects being the genuine appreciation we gain for experiences we used to take for granted.

A perfect example: A long-standing tradition in our home grants me Mother's Day eve off to do whatever I please. Does "whatever I please" usually consist of eating a meal in peace and quiet, doing returns at three different stores without a gaggle of "helpers" in tow, and shopping for new plants if I get especially adventurous? Yes, it does. It would be an utterly ho-hum outing before children. But it becomes a genuine treat once you've done enough errands during which the baby blows out his diaper or the toddler won't stop licking the escalator handrail.

It's not *better*. But you still appreciate it more. See? *Perspective.*

One of my favorite memories from our European adventure was a solo jaunt down the Champs-Élysées in Paris the evening before Mother's Day. You might say experiencing this tradition on one of the most glamorous streets in one of the most lauded cities in the world was a slight upgrade from my usual wander through Goodwill or Lowe's. And as I perched on a bench, enjoying a newly rain-washed landscape, people-watching, and consuming what was certainly the most delicious sandwich ever made, followed by the most decadent white chocolate tart on earth (courtesy of the gourmet chefs at Pomme de Pain, a French fast-food chain), I couldn't stop smiling. The sheer "I can't believe I get to do this" factor was so high that it elevated what a Parisian native would certainly have considered completely ordinary into a truly transcendent experience.

Knowing this opportunity to recharge meant that my precious family was waiting for me when I returned made it all the better.

My appreciation for that solo moment was not at odds with the joy I felt when some of my children—who have watched the film *The Sound of Music* too many times, if that's possible—began belting out the title song as we frolicked through the Swiss Alps one afternoon. The hills were, indeed, alive with wildflowers bobbing their friendly faces in the breeze, gentle cows waggling their shaggy heads, setting their neck bells ringing, and the sound of happy children echoing between snow-tipped peaks. And I was so glad all the people I love most were there to make the experience that much richer.

Shaun and I took a hot-air balloon ride on our honeymoon twenty years ago. I remember liking it. But the hot-air balloon ride we took with seven of our children during which our eight-year-old son, Theo, got to adjust the flame to steer the balloon? That I *loved.* And I will never forget the way the sun glinted off the not-quite-a-man-but-not-still-a-boy stubble on my teen sons' chins as they gazed with shining eyes over the Loire Valley.

I could give you example after example of ways having our children on that trip enhanced, not ruined, the experience. But I hope you get the point.

The key in every circumstance is perspective, yes, but also contentment.

THE KEY IN EVERY CIRCUMSTANCE IS PERSPECTIVE, YES, BUT ALSO CONTENTMENT.

Peace at All Times

On a hike to the Fairy Pools of the Isle of Skye in Scotland during an anniversary trip a year after our big family adventure, Shaun and I blew past a young family with three small children picking their way up the path. I overheard the father call good-naturedly to his daughter, who stooped down to peer at perfectly ordinary pebbles on the ground, "Come on, my little geologist. Let's keep moving."

Onward Shaun and I marched, pausing to appreciate the pools, then weaving our way between strolling tourists until we reached a particular photo opportunity he'd had in mind. And then back down we tramped. Well into our return hike, we encountered the young family again, still working their way up the path at a turtle's pace, stopping to appreciate every flower, every rock, every sparkling puddle.

Shaun and I locked eyes, not in relief we could move so much more quickly but in recognition. We know exactly what it feels like to adjust your settings to "wander, sniff, touch" and that it has a charm of its own.

For a moment, I felt a throb of regret that our kids weren't with us. And then I remembered this benediction from 2 Thessalonians 3:16: "Now may the Lord himself give you peace at all times in every way." I truly believe many of life's best moments involve our children—that their energy, wonder, and viewpoints add layers of depth and appreciation to even simple joys. But if we are granted the gift of time away, either alone or with our spouse, we're not experiencing "peace at all times in every way" if we spend it feeling unwarranted guilt for the break or wishing our situation were different. Instead, we miss out on the opportunity to experience the peace of God and give thanks in *all* circumstances.

Likewise, when we bemoan the limitations that children at times impose on an experience, rather than looking for the ways in which they add value (and stretch our capacity for growth), we bypass a chance to "rejoice always."

Which brings us all the way back to our internet friend and her "complicated" relationship with the prospect of having children.

No, I do not believe children "destroy" anything truly important (after all, we can't take a trim waistline, a job promotion, or even a perfectly ordered brain to heaven with us). Neither do I believe they must be present for an experience to have meaning.

Instead, they represent one of the richest opportunities—to die to self, to disciple well, to love God and love people, to humble ourselves and *become like them* in their trusting acceptance of their Father, that we may "enter the kingdom of heaven" (Matthew 18:3).

It's a prospect rife with both the simplicity of human connection and the complexity of finding ultimate worth in eternal things, which neither shining career paths nor perky figures nor impeccable memory recall can ever surpass.

A Titus Two Perspective

HEIDI ST. JOHN

author, speaker, podcast host, mother of seven

I was so thankful when Abbie called to ask if I would contribute to her new book because, as the mother of seven, I relate all too well to the myriad of emotional and physical realities of bearing children. My husband and I were married when I was nineteen and he was twenty-one. Our first child, who was born exactly two years into our marriage, gave me nearly *all* my stretch marks, along with a revised belly button that never seemed to recover from its turkey timer phase. Twenty years later, our seventh baby was born. When she was two years old, she glanced at my stomach after we finished a swimming lesson and exclaimed for all the locker room to hear, "Mama, why do you have a shiny star on your tummy?"

Of course, she didn't know the half of it. She was unaware that I was just weeks away from a surgery that would bring my childbearing years to an abrupt end. Uterine prolapse and years of pelvic floor "distress" had necessitated the need for bladder reconstruction and a hysterectomy. The surgery was difficult, and the recovery was grueling. But then again, doctors had warned me that it would be.

By the time we became pregnant with our seventh baby at the age of forty-one, we had counted the cost. We knew that more sleepless nights would be part of the deal. We knew what we were signing up for. We knew that eventually, my body was going to wave the white flag and surrender to a painful combination of age and injury. Yes, we knew what might be required—and knowing this, we joyfully welcomed our seventh baby into our hearts and home. We did this because we had something in our forties that we lacked in our twenties: We had the gift of perspective.

Precious mama, lean in—because you need to hear this:

The beautiful surrender that motherhood requires is worth it. In exchange for stretch marks, I have been given the gift of seven souls who have become my dearest and most trusted friends. I would not trade one sleepless night, one argument with a hormonal teenager, or all the years of financial struggle if it meant giving up the chance to love even one of these beautiful human beings who call me Mom.

The sleepless nights (at least those relating to little ones) are over now. All but one of our seven children have left the nest that I have spent my entire adult life feathering. My kitchen stays a little cleaner for a little longer. I can sleep in again on a Saturday if I want to, and my checkbook is a little less stressed than it used to be—and I would do it all again.

Maybe you need a little perspective today, so I hope this "older mama" can give you just enough to make the hard work you are doing seem a little more doable today. Motherhood is worth it. It's true that these days will go by faster than you can imagine—and when you look back, you'll smile at those "shiny stars" on your belly. The blessing of motherhood is obvious from the first look at a beautiful newborn but is never fully realized until you look into the eyes of your beautiful adult children. The mystery of motherhood is both profound and simple: It starts in love, grows with time, and matures with grace. The sleepless nights won't last forever, but the love that motherhood offers you, well, it will.

The Narrative

A WORLDLY RESPONSE TO "WORTH IT"	A BIBLICAL RESPONSE TO "WORTH IT"
Allows fear of "what if" to dictate her view of having children	Knows that children are a blessing and a gift from the Lord
Views childbearing as something akin to an illness	Sees the ability to bear children as a unique and precious privilege
Thinks it's impossible to enjoy activities and experiences as much as she did before she had children	Believes life's adventures are ultimately made better by having children along for the ride

Action Steps

- Memorize and meditate on 2 Corinthians 4:8-9: "We are afflicted in every way, but not crushed; perplexed, but not driven to despair; persecuted, but not forsaken; struck down, but not destroyed."
- Take a moment to acknowledge the ways that motherhood has altered your body, mind, and soul.
- Now compare those changes to the improvements you've noticed in all three of those areas since having children. Hint: Sometimes, they'll line up; sometimes, there will be a discrepancy. That's okay! It's good to notice, acknowledge, and give thanks where we can.

Questions

What are the world's standards for claiming that motherhood "destroys" us?

What does the Bible have to say about the changes that motherhood (or any challenging circumstance) brings about in us?

What is one way you've changed since becoming a mother for which you can thank God?

Prayer

Jesus, thank You that You allowed Yourself to truly be destroyed (for a time) for our benefit. Help us to have eyes of gratitude to see the changes inevitably wrought within us by motherhood as opportunities to share in Your sufferings and Your joys. Amen.

CHAPTER 5

If It Makes Us More like Jesus

It might seem a little late, four chapters in, to define our terms when it comes to the phrase "worth it," but before we wade any deeper into the merits of motherhood, I feel I should make my intent clear. Because what may seem "worth it" to some might not to others in a variety of scenarios.

Take bungee jumping, for example. I've been paragliding (not to mention hot-air ballooning) and loved every moment of it. I'm hoping my son Simon makes good on his promise to take me skydiving when he turns eighteen in a few months.

Clearly, I am not afraid of heights.

But plummeting from said heights headfirst, attached only by my feet to a stretchy rope anchored to a bridge? Nothing but the very salvation of someone I love from imminent death could make this choice "worth it" to me. I don't enjoy the feeling of my innards trading places with each other, thank you very much. Or what about free solo climbing the sheer cliff face of a mountain? I know some find this exhilarating and well worth the risk. I do not. The same goes for training for an ultramarathon or climbing Mount Everest.

They're all a bit too extreme for my tastes.

Which is funny because I am fully aware that quite a few consider my choice to be open to many children just as drastic. Never mind that I never actively tried to birth ten children in fourteen years. I'm here now, by God's grace. And the way in which expressions morph from bland expectancy to pop-eyed shock when I answer the question "And how many children do you have?" is something I've come to anticipate with a ready smile and an enthusiastic "Yep, TEN. And we love it!"

Many believe I have chosen to engage in "extreme parenting," and they hold the same view of our situation as I do of the man who hikes off into the wilderness with nothing but a sleeping bag, a canteen, and the hope of finding some lizards to eat for dinner. "Okay for her," they say. "But nothing could make that worth it to me."

(Truly, "better you than me" is a consistent theme.)

So, what *does* make parenting children (of any number) worth the effort? Because, while yes, it is more work to parent ten times as many, one child still requires great sacrifice, attention, and care.

Is it the crooked-lettered cards on our birthdays declaring us "the best mama I ever had"? Is it the dimpled hand tightly gripping ours as we climb the stairs each night? Is it the pride bursting in our chests when they whack a home run or cross the stage and solemnly shift the tassel from one side of their graduation cap to the other?

Is it the milestones and the breakthroughs and the moments of pure connection?

I think the answer is yes.

And no.

To illustrate the first response, I'll share two of my favorite "momming older kids" stories to date (with permission from both parties).

Taking the Shot

A couple of years ago, my son Simon joined our homeschool league's basketball team. He'd only played casually on Wednesday nights after church before signing up for the league, but he was determined to improve *pronto*. He spent hours every day drilling, shooting, dribbling, and feinting. And his hard work paid off because the contrast between his first and last game of the season was pronounced.

One night near the end of the season after we'd had a chat about some attitude adjustments that needed to happen, I ended the conversation with "I love you, Simon. Go splash me some threes tomorrow." I'd intended to lift the serious mood, but it crashed back down as he mumbled, "I can't."

"Why do you say that?" I asked.

"Because when I shot a three during yesterday's game and missed, Coach yelled at me to never try that again."

Y'all. That got this Texan mama's dander right up.

Swallowing an angry retort, I forced my voice to be calm as I said, "Simon, your coach gets carried away sometimes. I know he means well, but this is not his best advice. Just because you don't get something right the first time doesn't mean you stop trying. This is your first year, and you have lots of room for growth. Keep practicing. I think you're perfectly capable of making any shot if you'll just try. Now go get some sleep."

It wasn't going to win any awards for "most inspiring speech," but as he lifted his gaze from the ground, the corner of his mouth twitched in a grin. "Night, Mama," he said, heading for the door. Just before it shut behind him, he added, "Maybe I'll get you a three tomorrow."

As I watched his game the next day, I hadn't forgotten about this exchange, but I did doubt he'd risk the embarrassment of failure on the court again so soon.

I was happy to be wrong.

Halfway through the game, a teammate tossed him the ball at the top of the three-point line, and I held my breath as, without a beat of hesitation, he took the shot.

It wasn't pretty. It barreled toward the basket, flat as a day-old Coca-Cola, and my eyes tracked its trajectory in slow motion, willing it to clear the rim.

Before I could release my breath, it was over. Seemingly against all laws of physics, the ball pinged off the back rim and into the net. *He'd made the shot!*

Instantly, both my fists were in the air as I bellowed "THAT'S MY BOY!!" not caring whose eardrums I might rupture.

And then? He turned and raced down the court toward the opposite end with the rest of his team, incandescent with victory, and as he ran, he pointed straight at me.

That one was for you, Mama.

Friends, if the theme to *Hoosiers* had begun playing over the loudspeakers that very moment, it could not have added to my joy. No sports movie with its euphoric scenes of underdog defiance, ecstatic team hugs set to soaring scores, and fist pumps of triumph could hold the dimmest candle to the magic of the moment my son made his first three-pointer when, just the night before, he'd said, "I can't."

Choking back sobs, I picked up the twinbie I'd dumped in an unceremonious heap on the floor when I started screaming, and I hugged him tight. He held my face in his hands, confused by the tears leaking out of his mama's eyes as she beamed like a fool. When I asked Shaun later if it was silly that this might be one of the most core memories of my life, he said, "I don't think so at all."

It wasn't simply pride for my son's willingness to try again. It was the affirmation that "wise words satisfy like a good meal; the right words bring satisfaction" (Proverbs 18:20 NLT). That our encouragement matters. That motherhood is not merely shoveling sand from one pile to another and then back again. I know it isn't. And yet, in the daily grind of signing school releases and slapping together PB&Js, it can be easy to assume the words we say pass like water through the sieves of our children's busy brains, leaving nothing but microscopic sediment behind.

That three-pointer was so much more than a moment of sports glory. It was an Ebenezer of "worth it" to a weary mama's soul (not to mention a boost of confidence to a young man's spirit). And I will always be grateful to God for the way that leather ball banged into that metal hoop on a perfectly ordinary Thursday afternoon.

As obvious a "worth it" as that moment was, the next example might be even more gratifying. But first, I'll need to travel back in time for a bit of context.

A Pivotal Pivot

When I found myself in the throes of postpartum rage after Shiloh's birth (manifested as hormonal irritability, harsh words, faultfinding, and overreactions), my oldest, Ezra, was on the cusp of adolescence. Preteen boys can be delightful, but it's also a tricky age as they navigate burgeoning hormones, changing physiques, and the myriad subtle tweaks we must make to our relationships as they begin their passage from boyhood to manhood.

Ezra has been an old soul since age five—observant, conscientious, even-tempered, thoughtful.

But he has also inherited a trait both Shaun and I have to battle within ourselves: a critical spirit. "Noticing" can easily turn into "judging," and if an adult who has walked with the Lord for many years sometimes struggles in this area, it only makes sense that a twelve-year-old baby Christian would do the same.

When the Lord gave me the idea for the Gentleness Challenge (which I describe at length in *M Is for Mama*), I asked Ezra to help hold me accountable because I knew he would follow through. And so began thirty days of holding my tongue, choosing kind words, and apologizing immediately when I failed. Ezra kept his end of the bargain with calm reminders when needed, and I could tell he noticed the difference in me. But I could also see his struggle to let go of past transgressions. It was a topic of prayer between me and the Lord during the months that followed as I made life-giving speech a central focus of growth throughout 2019.

God was faithful to help me develop lasting habits in this area and to help Ezra mature in forgiveness and compassion for his mama. And as the years progressed, our relationship not only deepened but continued to broaden from parent/child to mentor/mentee. In January of 2023, I started a podcast. Thanks to a talent for technology he *definitely* inherited from Shaun, Ezra helped me launch it, and I hired him as my editor and producer. Was the transition without hiccups? Definitely not. But as we worked through each bump together, our relationship shifted yet again. Mother, mentor, employer, and now friend.

That summer, Shaun, Ezra, and I discovered the wonderful world of pickleball and all fell deeply in love with the sport. Anyone who has read my other books or followed along on social media for a while knows Thursday has been date night for as long as Shaun and I have been together. So, when our advanced pickleball round-robin got switched to that very night, we found ourselves faced with a choice: skip pickleball and stick with traditional date night or pivot and establish a new routine.

We chose the latter and began a regular habit of playing pickleball with Ezra (and others) each Thursday night, then going out to eat with him after we finished. And you know what? We all loved it. I can't recommend investing in your older teens enough, even if it means giving up something you love for a season (because they'll soon be full-fledged adults with busy social schedules and new priorities).

Which brings us all the way to Mother's Day of 2024. Every Mother's Day, during breakfast, each of my children hands me a note, and while I adore this tradition, it's also true that, through age nine or so, most of their hand-scrawled letters express sentiments similar to the "best mama I ever had" variety I mentioned previously.

Not all make it into the drawer I reserve for my dearest motherhood treasures. But that year, Ezra wrote me a letter that included the following, and you bet your stretch marks it's going in the vault forever:

"But more important than any other title or position you have, you are our mama, and what an excellent mama you are, patient to clean up the latest brown Jackson Pollock–like masterpiece from the nursery, willing to give the last of your Izze to the twinbie undoubtedly asking for it, happy to help whichever child is stuck on his math problem, always offering wise instruction to each and every one of us. You get up every day ready to pour your heart into us and we love you for it (Proverbs 31:28: 'Her children rise up and call her blessed')."

"Her children rise up and call her blessed."
(Proverbs 31:28)

It's a good thing I'm not scratching this chapter out using physical paper and ink, else these words would be blurred with tears as I write.

How do you know if all the effort is worth it? Well, you find yourself in a hard place of self-reflection—a mirror of your faults in your firstborn's eyes—and you ask the Lord to give you the strength to change. And then you watch Him draw you both to Himself, bit by bit, polishing away the sharp angles and rough patches until the final shape begins to become clear. We're never perfectly smooth and shapely this side of glory. But the progress? The growth?

Worth every moment of struggle and more.

We're never perfectly smooth and shapely this side of glory. But the progress? The growth? Worth every moment of struggle and more.

A Road Filled with Potholes

I told you I'd share these stories as obvious examples of "mama highlights"—resounding exclamation points to the question of what makes the relentless investment of motherhood worth it. But I believe they represent only one aspect of the answer.

To round out the picture, let me tell you a different story. I could do so from my own experience, but I believe this example, from a mother of multiple adult children older than my own, illustrates my point better.

A dear friend I admire so much has stumbled down a pothole-filled road of motherhood over the last several years with one of her grown children. While all the details are not mine to share, I know enough of the situation to vouch for the pain and betrayal this mama has endured and the faithfulness of the Lord to which she has clung.

Lest your brain wander to questions of "what she did wrong" (mine can do the same in similar situations, mostly because I want a formula for "what to avoid"), I want to assure you that I know few who are more devoted to their children, few who have invested more intentionally in their spiritual training and growth. Did she blunder or fail at times? Well, she must have because "all have sinned and fall short of the glory of God" (Romans 3:23).

But she prayed faithfully, loved relentlessly, and never wavered in her confidence in the goodness of her heavenly Father.

At the time that I type these words, she remains unreconciled to her wayward child, despite continued efforts and fervent prayer on her part. So was all her devotion wasted if all her children have not "turned out" like she hoped?

The One Who Never Sinned

To discover the answer, we have only to look to the Man of Sorrows Himself, Jesus. Though never a parent, He spends three years pouring wisdom and spiritual nourishment into twelve men whom the world would have deemed unworthy of His efforts. Fishermen and tax collectors, lowly and despised by society, they nevertheless receive instruction from the mouth of God Himself. Contrary to every other teacher (or parent), Christ never stumbles, never misspeaks, never sins.

And how do these privileged chosen few respond when put to the test?

They fall asleep during Jesus's greatest hour of need, and when evil men wrongfully arrest Him, "all the disciples deserted Him and fled" (Matthew 26:56 BSB).

Not only that, but Peter—so bold and full of his own virtue he declares, "Even if all fall away on account of You, I never will" (Matthew 26:33 BSB)—denies any connection with Jesus not once, not twice, but three times mere hours later (Matthew 26:69-75).

We could hardly blame Jesus if He were to wash His hands of this ragtag bunch of turncoats in disgust. But He doesn't. Instead, when for the third time Peter insists he doesn't know his Lord, Jesus merely turns and looks at him, a gaze so piercing it reduces Peter to bitter tears (Luke 22:61-62). And as Jesus hangs on the cross, racked with agony, splayed in humiliation for the mockery of His enemies, He speaks tenderly to John, whom the Bible calls "beloved" by the Lord. He entrusts Mary to him, saying, "'Here is your mother,'" and the passage tells us, "from then on this disciple took her into his home" (John 19:27 NLT).

When our children fail us, abandon us, betray us, is our first instinct to trust them again? To give them responsibility or privileges? I know my answer is often no. And yet Jesus chooses to forgive, to nudge toward repentance with a glance, to humble Himself to the point of death for the very ones who abandoned Him (Philippians 2:8). He chooses to see worth, even without evident or immediate return, in His sacrifice for humanity.

Why?

Because He wasn't doing it for recognition or acclaim. He wasn't doing it so we would "act right" or "make Him look good." He did it to fulfill the will of His Father, for the redemption of mankind, and with the mindset of an eternity seated at the right hand of God the Father reigning in majesty and dominion forever.

Clearly, a mere mortal's motivation for parenting well will diverge from that of the Son of God's purpose in dying for the sins of the world. And yet there are crucial parallels here.

After all, it's not "Lord, give all my kids successful and happy lives" but "Lord, please reveal my children's sin and desperate need for You and protect them from the evil one" (see John 17:15). And it's less "Give me moments of emotional victory" and more "Thy will be done" (see Matthew 6:10).

The moments of victory? They're awfully nice. They help sustain us through seasons of struggle. But my friend whose child has strayed will be the first to tell you who truly sustains her.

She will also be the first to admit that, though unpleasant, the conflict with her adult child has forced a deeper reliance on God and a greater love for His Word. The way she weaves Scripture through her everyday conversation leaves me in awe of her intimate knowledge of its truths, hungry to learn more for myself.

And I'm convicted to my core when I hear her say that being reviled without

MOTHERHOOD IS WORTH IT
IF IT MAKES US MORE LIKE JESUS.

any recourse to "clear her name" to her accusers has helped her better understand the sufferings of Christ. Not only that, but she's learned to let go of what others think—even those whom she considered friends in the past.

"It's not fun," she confesses. "But it's given me more fear of God and less of man."

And that, my friends, is truly the answer to what makes this whole motherhood endeavor worth it.

Is it worth it when it feels warm and fuzzy? Sure.

Is it worth it when we can see a change of heart? Absolutely.

Is it worth it when the relationship continues, untarnished by resentment or broken connection? Yep.

None of these things is inherently ungodly or unworthy.

Yet they all fall short of this one unchanging standard.

It's worth it—even when it doesn't feel good—if it makes us more like Jesus.

A Titus Two Perspective

TAMMY CANNON

mother of eight

I am the mom whom Abbie referred to in this chapter. My husband and I have been happily married for over thirty years, and we have eight children. I have the privilege of knowing Abbie through various activities with our kids and watching her live out what she shares. In fact, it was at one of these activities that she and I were discussing trials with adult children and how the Lord can use them for good.

When the situation with my adult child first occurred, I thought, "What was the point of all the effort I poured into my children if they are just going to walk away from everything?"

Is it worth it if I do not see the results in my children that I had prayed for and intentionally worked toward?

It is if I have an eternal perspective.

"Whatever you do, work heartily, as for the Lord and not for men, knowing that from the Lord you will receive the inheritance as your reward. You are serving the Lord Christ" (Colossians 3:23-24).

I had memorized this as a reminder that my work as a mom is to be done with all my heart as serving the Lord, and that it would be worth it before Him, regardless of the outcome.

I have learned that it is not about whether my children reject the Lord and His ways, or about me being a perfect parent, but about me being obedient and entrusting my children to the One who works in their hearts as He works in mine.

When the parenting season is over, I need to rest in knowing that I have done my job and leave the results to God. After all, we only plant and water—He makes it grow (1 Corinthians 3:6-7).

Early on in the situation with my adult child, my mom told me that even if my child never turns around, the Lord can still use this for good in me.

"And we know that all things work together for good to those who love God…For whom He foreknew, He also predestined *to be* conformed to the image of His Son" (Romans 8:28-29, NKJV).

So, it is worth it if it makes me more like Jesus.

Jesus "learned obedience from the things He suffered" (Hebrews 5:8, NLT). And I can truly testify to the truth of Psalm 119:71: "It was good for me to be afflicted, that I might learn Your statutes" (BSB). Although I would not have chosen this situation with our adult child, I am thankful for it as it has refined me and drawn me closer to the Lord and His Word in a way like never before, causing me to live by faith in a good God whom I cannot see instead of by my circumstances that I can see.

May this trial of my faith "result in praise, glory and honor when Jesus Christ is revealed" (1 Peter 1:7 NIV).

The Narrative

A WORLDLY RESPONSE TO "WORTH IT"	A BIBLICAL RESPONSE TO "WORTH IT"
Thinks motherhood should be a highlight reel	Thanks God in moments of euphoria *and* struggle
Looks for the "happy ending"	Finds comfort in God's sovereignty, regardless of the outcome
Banks on "results" from her children after years of expended effort	Acknowledges the "result" that matters most is a more Christlike heart and mind

Action Steps

- Memorize and meditate on Philippians 2:8: "And being found in human form, he humbled himself by becoming obedient to the point of death, even death on a cross."
- List at least two "motherhood highlights" that come to mind (they don't have to be momentous, just important to you). Take a moment to thank God for them.
- List at least two motherhood struggles that are pushing you closer to the Lord. Take a moment to thank God for them.

Questions

What in your life has shaped your character to be more like Jesus's: triumphs or struggles? Why?

What are some of the pitfalls of performative parenting, which assures us it's "worth it" only when we get the "results" we want in our kids?

How do the heartaches of parenting equip us to help others who struggle?

Prayer

Lord, thank You that You allow us to experience moments of both joy and sorrow in parenting. May we have clear eyes of humility to recognize You are the Giver of all good things, even when they don't feel good at the moment. Teach us to rejoice in all circumstances. Amen.

CHAPTER 6

You Only Spill What's Already Inside

I can almost hear the throat clears and see the raised fingers of hundreds of mamas who read the last sentence of the last chapter and would like to enter the chat: "Okay, but what if I *don't* feel like all this mental, emotional, and physical expenditure *is* making me more like Jesus? What if motherhood is actually making me angrier and less patient? What then?"

It's a fair point. One of the most frequently asked questions every week on Whaddya Wanna Know Wednesday (WWKW, a Q&A on my Instagram account @m.is.for.mama) is "How do I deal with mom rage? I thought I was a patient person until I had kids."

I've heard my fair share of "My children make me crazy, angry, frustrated, anxious, ______________." And while I try to avoid using this phrasing out loud, I sometimes find myself gravitating toward this mindset as well, especially when I'm tired or overwhelmed.

The problem with "they make me" is that it robs the adults in the equation (that's us, friends!) of all agency and places the onus of "behaving well so Mama can stay sane" upon our children.

I'll dive into the behavioral aspect of this topic soon, but first I want to highlight an illustration I heard in a talk by pastor, speaker, and award-winning author, Paul Tripp.

Imagine yourself holding a water bottle without the lid on. Somebody walks by and jostles you, sloshing water down your front despite your best efforts to hold the bottle still.

Why did water come out of the bottle?

You might be tempted to say, "Because she bumped me."

Somewhat true, but what if I change the emphasis? Why did *water* come out of the bottle (instead of something else)?

The answer, of course, is because water was already in the bottle.

A bottle of water can't overflow with coffee, tea, or hot chocolate, because its contents have been predetermined and can't be changed by a collision with another human being.[1]

The New Living Translation succinctly puts it this way: "What you say flows from what is in your heart" (Luke 6:45), and Proverbs 4:23 says, "Keep your heart with all vigilance, for from it flow the springs of life."

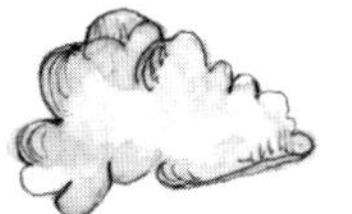

"What you say flows from what is in your heart." (Luke 6:45)

So do your toddler's antics fill you with rage? The correct answer is: No, they don't.

The rage is already inside of you. Your small children are merely the vehicle God allowed to smash into your expectations and your sleep deprivation and your (ahem, *my*) selfishness. The same holds true of your teenager. If his consistent failure to come home at curfew results in your ranting and a tailspin of insults and angry ultimatums, his wrong behavior did not cause your poor response. It merely revealed the capacity for such a response that has existed within you all along.

Even Jesus Grew Weary

Anytime I speak on this topic, I typically get two objections. The first usually goes something like this: "I don't like where this is going. Are you telling me that getting upset when my kids sin is *never* okay?"

I'll answer with this account from Mark 3:1-5: "Again he [Jesus] entered the synagogue, and a man was there with a withered hand. And they watched Jesus, to see whether he would heal him on the Sabbath, so that they might accuse him...And he said to them, 'Is it lawful on the Sabbath to do good or to do harm, to save life or to kill?' But they were silent. And he looked around at them with anger, grieved at their hardness of heart."

This is God incarnate, utterly sinless and completely holy. And His response to the callousness of the Pharisees is grief and anger. No, your kids can't *make* you sin. That's on you. But a natural uprising of emotion in response to *their* sin is appropriate. It's what we do with this response that marks the difference between whether the interaction reflects the work of the Holy Spirit in our lives or is, instead, an outflow of our flesh.

Take heart, mamas. Simply feeling frustrated at behavior that would try the patience of a saint (if you are in Christ, you *are* one!) does not mean motherhood is making you less like Jesus.

In fact, the English Standard Version of Ephesians 4:26 takes this concept a step further when it says, "Be angry and do not sin." In other words, the problem lies not in the emotions you feel stirring within you but in the sinful ways such emotions are often expressed.

We must learn to embrace the fact that negative emotions will likely arise when we encounter struggle (or plain old defiance), but this does not absolve our responsibility to surrender both our feelings and our desire for control to God so He can give us His supernatural self-control in return. What a worthwhile trade-off!

An Unexpected Gift

The second point that people get hung up on is this: "You said it's worth it if it *makes* us more like Jesus. If the circumstances that drive us bonkers only uncover the impatient character within, wouldn't that mean the ones that 'make us more like Jesus' are revealing some sort of goodness within, if that's what comes out as a result?"

Not exactly.

Perhaps a more accurate phrasing of the sentiment would be this: "Each effort in motherhood—life, really—is worth it if it reveals our need for our Savior, and we turn to Him for help." After all, the Lord alone is the One who frees us from our bondage to self.

Each effort in motherhood—life, really—is worth it if it reveals our need for our Savior, and we turn to Him for help.

Second Corinthians 3:16-18 puts it like this: "But when one turns to the Lord, the veil is removed. Now the Lord is the Spirit, and where the Spirit of the Lord is, there is freedom. And we all, with unveiled face, beholding the glory of the Lord, are being transformed into the same image from one degree of glory to another."

Did you catch the phrase "are being transformed"?

It's a process, not an instant personality flip. So if you feel that motherhood "makes you" less like Jesus every day, know this: The revelation that you're not as patient or self-controlled or organized or kind as you initially imagined you were is a gift. Why? Because without that self-awareness, we might keep blundering down the same dark paths of rage, resentment, and self-pity without realizing there's a way out that leads to the light of godly repentance and change.

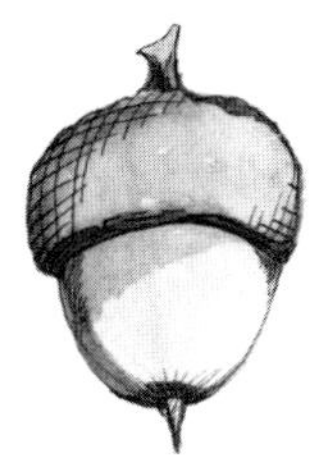

The revelation that you're not as patient or self-controlled or organized or kind as you initially imagined you were is a gift.

Understandably, many of us (myself included, at times) would prefer that gift resemble an instantaneous infusion of character development rather than the painstaking three-steps-forward-two-steps-back process that often characterizes sanctification through motherhood. We would be happy to have a moment similar to the one Neo from *The Matrix* experiences when he "learns" martial arts. After being hooked up to a computer via a gnarly-looking spike inserted into a port at the base of his skull (I'll skip that part, thanks), he wonders aloud, "Jujitsu. I'm going to learn...jujitsu?" The answer is, not really. The movie speeds through a sequence of Neo's fitful semiconsciousness as various fight disciplines are uploaded to his brain, no training or practice required. When he awakens, he displays an impressive mastery of everything from, yes, jujitsu to kung fu and more.

This, my friends, is what we think we want when we ask God for an indwelling of His Holy Spirit. But this earthly life is no action movie montage. Chances are, when you beg the Lord for patience, you receive not a heavenly basket of the fruit of the Spirit at your doorstep, but a 2:00 a.m. wakeup from a toddler who proudly announces, "I poop on the potty!"

Problem is, you know you've been way too exhausted to start potty training yet, and when you walk into the blinding glare of the fluorescent lights, rubbing grit from your eyes, and behold the sheer volume of brown on the walls, patience feels as far away as that last shred of sleep you'd love to reclaim. And yet this scenario, along with a thousand others, is exactly the classroom in which we learn to pursue true growth, rather than crossing our fingers and hoping for the best (and then pouting when it doesn't materialize).

Professional
DEVELOPMENT

Built-in Professional Development

I distinctly remember one morning when my sister-in-law called right after breakfast.

"How's your morning been, sis?"

"Oh, man," I said. "A bit touch and go."

"Oh yeah? What happened?"

"Well," I said, thinking through the previous thirty minutes, "I fed five little boys breakfast…"

When I didn't go on, she said, "Uh-oh, what happened?"

"Oh, no. Nothing happened," I clarified with a laugh. "That was the whole story—breakfast for five little boys. Phew! We made it!"

My guess is you can relate. Even the "simple" act of making scrambled eggs for your small children can sometimes feel like an epic quest through a minefield of "Help you, Mama?" and "Careful, it's hot!" and "Yes, it's almost ready!" One toddler drags a chair over your toe in his haste to get to the off-limits burner. The five-year-old slops half the eggs on the floor in his determination to be of assistance, and the other toddler sits on the floor wailing in disconsolation that his brother thought of assaulting you with a chair first. Meanwhile, the older boys bicker about who gets to stir the eggs, assuming they ever make it in the pan.

I'm a seasoned mama of every age and stage, and every now and then I still walk away from breakfast feeling as if I've escaped with only a sliver of my dignity (and my toenail) intact. The difference is I now know these moments have inherent value in the built-in professional development they offer me as a mother. Where my twenty-five-year-old self might have stalked away from a muddled morning muttering, "What's the point?" I now feel confident the Lord has orchestrated just such a moment because, apparently, I need an opportunity to practice patience and "count it all joy" (James 1:2). Because practicing the fruit of the Spirit's indwelling in His strength is about the only guaranteed way to experience change, maturity, and the kind of joy that doesn't depend on your performance or your children's reactions to it.

Sadly, if we keep shoving away opportunities to rehearse the truths of Scripture in everyday, mundane scenarios, we're likely to grow—but in frustration, not in forbearance.

Don't Go Away Sad

Once, when I was speaking at a homeschool conference in another state, a mom of five approached my booth to chat. Soon, she was confiding in me her irritation at her twin boys' antics.

"I can't get anything done without their destroying everything. They get home from school, and I can't even make dinner in peace, because they're busy jumping on all the furniture and tossing the pillows across the room." (In fairness, "throw pillow" might not have been the wisest name if we didn't want this to happen.)

As a mama of seven males, including twin boys, I could relate. The couch cushions rarely stay put during dinner prep, and it's not uncommon for the leather poufs we use as footrests to be piled into precarious towers from which my sons leap with varying degrees of skill and safe landings.

I wasn't sure whether this mom wanted to simply vent her frustration or to look for solutions, but she was clearly struggling. So when she stopped to shake her head in despair, I suggested what I often do when moms struggle to complete tasks in the kitchen: "What if you invited your twins to help with dinner?"

Honestly, I might have gotten a better response if I'd suggested she serve skunk for dinner.

"I can't do that," she said, clearly horrified. "That would make it *worse*."

When I asked her why, she said, "Because then I really never would finish dinner."

I acknowledged, at the outset, it would make the dinner-prep process more challenging. "But just wait until they can grate cheese, whisk eggs, fry bacon, peel potatoes, and so much more," I said. "Not only will they have valuable life skills, but they'll also be occupied doing something productive while you make dinner. Your living room won't get trashed as often, and it will be great bonding time with them. Win-win-win-win!"

Her expression fell even further as she said, "Yeah, that would never work." I opened my mouth to assure her it could—that I knew this from years of doing this exact process with multiple children—but she had already begun to walk away in dejection. I couldn't help but think of the phrase from Matthew 19:22, which says the rich young ruler "went away sorrowful" after he heard Jesus's instructions to sell everything he owned and give it to the poor.

This frazzled mama and that wealthy man had something in common: They didn't find the sacrifice (of effort and resources) worth it for the long-term benefit, likely because they couldn't imagine their current circumstances changing in a beneficial enough way to warrant it. And this, my friends, is at the root of so many struggles we face when it *doesn't* feel like the results we're getting merit the effort. Every day, we bash our heads against the same walls of chaotic dinnertimes or sibling smackdowns, and we think, "This couldn't possibly be worth it. I'm exhausted, and these kids sure don't feel like the blessing the Bible tells me they are."

May I humbly suggest, if this is the case, it might be time to face the problem head-on, even if it requires great effort, rather than "going away sorrowful" again. I obviously don't know your particular struggles, but after chatting with countless harried mamas over the years, a couple of common themes have emerged, which I'll address in the next chapter.

For now, I leave you with this: You're not broken (or a "bad mom") if you get angry at your children. Or tire of caring for their endless needs. Or dread the constant bickering that seems to start before your eyes are even open and doesn't end until they close at night.

But you are a mom in need of hope.

You're not broken (or a "bad mom")
if you get angry at your children...
But you are a mom in need of hope.

I am thrilled to tell you hope has a name. It's Jesus, and He has come "that [you] may have life and have it abundantly" (John 10:10).

If that sounds better than what you're currently experiencing in motherhood, read on!

 "Keeping Them Close" Activities 

If you struggle to think of ways to allow your children to contribute meaningfully alongside you in your home, you are not alone!

Below is a brief list of some tried-and-true activities that help keep my children close with their brains and hands busy when they might otherwise be engaged more destructively.

Folding clothes while I read aloud to them

Whenever I share this "mom hack," at least one woman always responds, "Why didn't I think of this?" The simple genius of it is that you're combining a chore that must be done with education and entertainment all rolled into one.

"Scrubbing" jobs

If you need to get things done in the kitchen but have children you need close by and occupied who are too young to help chop or sauté, hand them a toothbrush and a bowl of soapy water. Then, let them scrub your kitchen cabinets to their heart's content. The same goes for wiping down refrigerators, cleaning nearby windows, or scouring the kitchen sink. You may not get a pro-level result, but the actual motions require few fine motor skills, and the practice (for them) and peace of mind (for you) are worth it.

Bonus: Your floors will be a little cleaner too, after you mop up the inevitable spill from the bowl.

Cooking classes

I have a child who thanks me for teaching him how to cook every single time we do our family tradition of going around the room on a birthday and saying what we love most about the honoree.

The thing is, I didn't give that much formal instruction or set aside a specific hour each week to teach him how to make scrambled eggs that don't stick to the pan. I simply invited him in to observe and participate in what I was already doing. This principle of welcoming your children to come *alongside you* is the best way to convey skills without feeling as if you must set up a time and day to do so. Because that will probably never happen.

Timers and speed cleans

Does it seem like nothing in your home ever stays clean? Welcome to motherhood! I encourage you to shift your mindset from a constant need for "global cleans" (which can overwhelm, causing you to put them off indefinitely) to targeted family speed cleans that allow you to effectively address a particular area that's been overrun by kid stuff, clutter, or grime. Make a list of the necessary tasks, assign them to your children in an age-appropriate way, pick a job for yourself, and get after it! The best part: It teaches your kids how to work with concentration and diligence on one task at a time.

Organizing tasks

Even my least orderly children can organize the junk drawer in our kitchen when its eclectic collection of pencils, batteries, Post-Its, and paper clips gets out whack—but only if I'm willing to give them some pointers about how to group like items and where each category goes. I can also check on their progress while I work on the dishes nearby.

A Titus Two Perspective

GRETA ESKRIDGE

author, speaker, podcast host, mother of four

Early in my parenting journey, I learned to apply the wisdom found in Proverbs 15:1 to my most frustrating interactions with my kids. It says, "A gentle answer turns away wrath, but a harsh word stirs up anger" (NIV). But I will be the first to admit that it was not easy to live out this wisdom. For example, my fleshly response to my three-year-old dropping the milk carton and splashing milk all over the kitchen was to get irritated and frustrated because he had just created more work for me. Or there was the time we were getting ready to go somewhere, and I thought everyone was ready to go and waiting for me by the front door. Instead, I found two small children playing in the mud pit in the backyard, and my frustrated and angry response was to slam the back door so hard that the window cracked. Yes, that really happened, and yes, my kids still bring it up to me twelve-plus years later.

My responses in both those circumstances were not what Proverbs 15:1 called me to. Instead of recognizing that it was indeed an annoyance but not the end of the world, I gave in to harshness and anger. What I have learned over the years is that the gentle answer I am called to give actually quells my own anger. This proverb is an invitation to practice the fruit of the Spirit, especially self-control, patience, peace, kindness, gentleness…oh, well, all of them!

As my kids have entered the teen years, I have found that parenting with this proverb in mind still applies, maybe even more than when they were toddlers. That's because the hormones raging through their bodies and mine often meet head-to-head in battle. My first inclination is to respond to their grumpy, moody, angry, irritable, or even weepy moods with my own measure of grumpy, moody, angry, irritable, or weepy. But again, I am called to practice self-control, peace, and kindness. When I do, it almost always results in those things being offered back to me.

What does that look like practically? When my daughter is grumpy at the silly antics of her three brothers, I can respond with, "Just get over it!" Or I can say, "Why don't I make you a cup of tea, and you can find a quiet spot to read until you feel like you can handle the crazy again?" And when my son is frustrated that circumstances didn't go his way and he wants to take it out by pestering his little brother, I can just say, "Knock it off!" Or I can suggest he go for a run or have a snack because taking care of his body helps his mind feel better. And in both circumstances, I usually also ask, "Can I pray for you right now?"

This kind of response takes more time, effort, and care on my part. Sometimes I'd rather not handle it that way. I am busy with other things, or I am simply overwhelmed by my own emotional state and don't want to deal with anyone else's emotions. What I find again and again, though, is that when I practice that self-control I am called to, I step closer to my kids' hearts. And in turn, all of us step closer to the heart of God. I want a heart filled with the fruit of the Spirit, even amid spilled milk, muddy clothes, and a house full of hormonally charged teens. And motherhood is giving me chance and chance again to practice it. Praise God!

The Narrative

A WORLDLY RESPONSE TO "WORTH IT"	A BIBLICAL RESPONSE TO "WORTH IT"
Blames circumstances for her own reaction	Takes responsibility for her own sin
Wishes she could just improve without effort	Knows that "faith without works is dead"
Backs away from opportunities for growth if they feel daunting	Leans into godly solutions, knowing the goal is becoming more like Jesus

Action Steps

- Memorize and meditate on Proverbs 4:23: "Keep your heart with all vigilance, for from it flow the springs of life."
- Take a few minutes to consider your personality, then write down five adjectives that describe you. Ask your spouse or a trusted friend for a list of three to five adjectives to describe you as well.
- Pray about and consider whether the personality traits you/your loved ones see in you are pleasing to God in your season of motherhood. Pick one problematic trait to pray about and ask the Lord for the wisdom and courage to change.

Questions

Were you surprised by your capacity for irritation and anger once you became a mom? Why or why not?

Do you think our culture's fixation on personality tests and self-categorization is healthy? Why or why not?

Are you sometimes tempted to assume that, if change doesn't happen immediately, it's not coming at all?

Prayer

Father, You know us inside and out—our capacity for kindness and rage, laziness and industry. And You love us enough to transform us through the power of Your Holy Spirit. Thank You for opportunities to recognize our sinful tendencies and become more like You each day as we mother our children to the glory of God. Amen.

CHAPTER 7

When You Don't Like Them and They're Not Nice

I'm aware we could tackle an endless number of "motherhood quandaries" in this chapter. However, I want to address two struggles that rear their ugly heads in my inbox time and again. Remember: My goal has never been to get you to "parent like Abbie." Rather, I want to point you to God's Word and encourage you to rely on His Spirit to guide you in your pursuit of Christlikeness.

As such, if you get only one thing from this chapter, let it be this: Sister, read your Bible! Even if you don't know where to start (may I suggest *The Bible Recap*'s one-year guide?). Even if you don't understand it (ask God for wisdom and insight; James 1:5 says He *will* grant it). Even if you think it's boring (y'all, I know Leviticus can feel like a slog, but when you begin to understand the Bible is *one story* from beginning to end, even the most head-scratchingly obscure passages can reveal something about the character of God).

With these important caveats out of the way, let's dive in!

One of my most frequently requested resources is a list of every verse I reference throughout the M Is for Mama motherhood trilogy. I heard your requests, took it one step further, and turned the list into an ebook called *Well-Versed*. It includes categories for common motherhood struggles or concerns (think: prayer, wisdom, fear, triumph, confidence in Christ, and more). Under each category, I've included pertinent verses from my books for quick reference in times of stress or uncertainty or to give you direction for a Bible memory focus. I pray this compilation will bless you in your pursuit to know and love Jesus more. You can find the *Well-Versed* ebook at misformama.net/product/well-versed-ebook.

Struggle 1: You Don't Enjoy Being Around Your Children

"What if I don't even like my children?" is an uncomfortable thing to say (or type), but it's hardly an uncommon sentiment. (In fact, it's so mainstream, we belt it out in that catchy Christmas tune that goes "Mom and Dad can hardly wait for school to start again.")

The good news is, I truly believe this struggle is less a reflection of some permanent flaw (in either them or you) and more indicative of practices that aren't serving your family well.

Yes, some kids' personalities will naturally mesh better with ours than others, but I can say with candor that I like, as well as love, all of my children. (The "like factor" may be stronger at some times than others, depending on circumstances, but the principle remains.) And the main reason for this stems from some very simple steps we've taken in our home to ensure mutual respect and consideration are consistently demonstrated by and toward everyone who lives here.

The very first thing we must do if we wish to enjoy our children is to view them rightly according to God's Word.

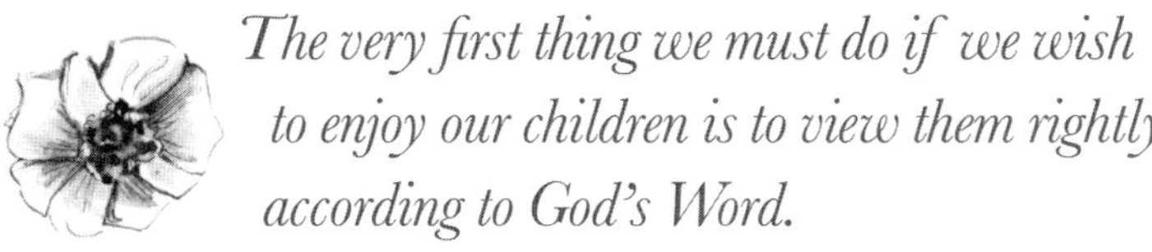

The very first thing we must do if we wish to enjoy our children is to view them rightly according to God's Word.

This primary truth sounds more theoretical than practical at first glance, but it has concrete benefits for us and our children. When we recognize children have inherent value as image-bearers of their Creator (Genesis 1:26), are fearfully and wonderfully knitted together by God even before they are born (Psalm 139:14), and are welcomed by Jesus (Mark 10:15-16), we can begin to shift our perspective from annoyance to acceptance and even appreciation.

Not only that, but when we heed Christ's example of "let the little children come to Me" (Matthew 19:14 BSB), we are forced to admit that Jesus made this standard without caveats. Not "let them come if they are quiet or clean or well behaved or cheerful." But simply, let them come.

I write this as four of my sons engage in what appears to be all-out warfare on our living room rug. As the teenager "attacks" his younger brothers with couch pillows and poufs, they squeal with delight, launching their small bodies at his well-muscled one, heedless of threat to frame or furniture. Everything in my female soul yearns to shout, "STOP!" And not simply because I'm having trouble concentrating on typing these words (if you've ever wondered how I get books written with so many children in the house, well, this is one of the answers). I flinch as curly heads collide with the padded ottoman, and I can't help but blurt, "Not so hard!" as Simon lifts a twinbie high above his head and faux-slams him down on the couch.

But I don't forbid it. I allow it because I know this is necessary and important behavior for boys and their development. They need to move, wrestle, grapple, and play. I even encourage it within reason because this is a way I can "let the little children come" instead of constantly sending them away. (Of note:

I also regularly say, "Okay! Enough! If you need to be loud and rambunctious, you can do it outside now!" It's called balance, y'all.) This is a way I can develop mutual "like" between us as they see me smiling at their shenanigans, and I see them reveling in the glory of being boys.

This example dovetails into a general principle of exercising reasonable expectations for our children. If we prize a quiet and tidy home so much that every baking session, every music practice, every dance party, every at-home spa is a threat to *our* peace, *our* order, and *our* domain, we will resent the perpetrators of these activities (and so many more).

Many moms have a hard time letting their kids simply be kids. "It's my greatest struggle," admitted one mom of five. "I love a clean, calm house so much. But I also know we're all happier when I relax my standards, and we can have some fun and make productive messes." (And if you're thinking, "My house standards are actually pretty low, but I just don't like being messed with"? The same principles of setting aside your preferences for the sake of following Jesus and loving your family apply.)

On the flip side of reasonable expectations for "kid behavior" are reasonable expectations for considerate behavior. If many moms become exasperated when their offspring do "offspringy" things that interrupt their peace, even more mothers lose their cool when their kids won't express their wishes politely or show basic consideration for the needs and feelings of others.

I'll admit it's not easy to enjoy presumptuous, pushy children. Nor am I keen on sending an adult into the world who thinks only of himself and communicates exclusively in grunts or age-specific slang. We are experiencing an unprecedented epidemic of abdication when it comes to parents' modeling, discipling, and instructing their children in speech, behavior, and thoughts that honor God and others before self. In fact, the idea of prioritizing one's own desires as the highest form of love and the wellspring from which all other charity springs is perpetuated in everything from allergy medication advertisements to sitcoms to social media.

"Love yourself, so you can love others," a cultured British voice-over purrs as a woman luxuriates in a bath, eating cookies while her children pound on the other side of a locked door. "Self-care first, period" barks another ad (which peddles a program that helps its users schedule out said "self-care" for every day of the month…for a small fee).

Just to give you a bit of mental whiplash, I'll throw out 1 Corinthians 10:24 as a contrast: "Let no one seek his own good, but the good of his neighbor."

Friends, this is not the same thing as "never take a shower, always give all your birthday treats to your kids, and only prioritize their preferences or desires." That's a short and certain road to burnout (for us) and entitlement (for them). But it *is* an acknowledgment that many of our priorities stem from an *already* elevated and cherished view of our own worth. The Bible never has to (and never does) remind us to be more self-focused. (This alone should pin a giant red flag on constant worldly encouragement to do so.) But biblical exhortations toward humility and other-centeredness abound *because we need them.*

The Bible never has to (and never does) remind us to be more self-focused. (This alone should pin a giant red flag on constant worldly encouragement to do so.)

And so do our children. Only by modeling a God-first, others-second, self-last approach (*and* explicitly teaching what that can look like on a practical, daily basis) will we hope to combat the current culture's aggressive and alluring messaging, which seeks to assure our kids that acting on their most selfish urges is not only natural but probably better for everyone in the long run.

If you're bothered by the progression of priorities I mentioned above, you'll have to take it up with Jesus, who said, "The last will be first" (Matthew 20:16), "for whoever wants to save his life will lose it; but whoever loses his life for My sake will find it" (Matthew 16:25 NASB), and "if anyone wants to come after

You Just Do.

Me, he must deny himself, take up his cross daily, and follow Me" (Luke 9:23 NASB).

I'll unpack the impact of the me-first fallacy more in future chapters, but I want to encourage you to stay strong on a course of encouraging and even *requiring* civility and consideration for others in your home, regardless of anyone else's standards.

You will benefit. Your children will benefit. Society will benefit. And you'll often find yourself grateful to be in the same room as your children, instead of wishing them away.

Some boots-on-the-ground suggestions to cultivate considerate kids:

Practice Politeness from an Early Age

"Please," "thank you," "yes, Mommy" (or, if you're Texans like we are, a crisp "yes ma'am"), "no, thank you," and "you're welcome" are phrases we start to teach as soon as our small children show an inclination to talk. Shaun and I are also constantly striving to model politeness in the way we speak to each other, to their siblings, and to others who enter our home.

In the same way smiling has been shown to increase your dopamine levels—improving your overall mood—speaking civil words helps shape the neural pathways of our brain toward conflict resolution instead of fight picking. Or, as neuroscientist Dr. Andrew Newberg and Mark Robert Waldman, a communications expert, note in their book *Words Can Change Your Brain*, "A single word has the power to influence the expression of genes that regulate physical and emotional stress."[1]

Proverbs 18:21 puts it like this: "Death and life are in the power of the tongue, and those who love it will eat its fruits."

The more we practice life-giving speech, the more naturally it flows. For us and our kids. Which is why we…

Outlaw Name-Calling and Derogatory Language

Yes, this is a continuation of point number one, and yes, I did say "outlaw." You may be wondering, "How do you establish an environment of civil speech in your home?" To some extent, the answer is "You just do" because you're the parent, and ain't nobody else gonna do it. It's not a one-and-done decision, though. And so much of the "how" has a hidden "How do I accomplish this without focusing on it *every single stinkin' day*?" element to it. It's a legitimate question because consistency is truly the star of the show here. It's worth the effort, though.

Practically, you have to decide the parameters for "civil speech" for your own family and be willing to follow them, repeat them, and enforce them. For our family, this means zero name-calling when our children are young—that includes "weirdo," "stupid," "meanie," the works. It doesn't mean everybody cooperates, but it does mean we all know the baseline from which we're operating, and there's no doubt that, *when* we fail, the goal is to restore trust and get back to that standard of kind speech—not out of legalism or fear but because we know it's right and reflects the way we, ourselves, want to be treated, just like it says in Matthew 7:12 (better known as the Golden Rule).

We can accomplish this by addressing unkind speech right away (instead of waiting to see if it will escalate), quickly separating parties whose angry emotions are overflowing in insults and attacks, and even applying a consequence if the parties involved refuse to listen to calm instructions to consider and correct their speech.

If you're hung up on that "when our children are young" bit, just know that, while I find strong, clear standards and swift, specific follow-through essential to establishing a consistent tone in the family home, there's also room for nuance as our kids mature. A perfect example: Once, when my then-thirteen-year-old daughter professed her love for root beer (which I loathe), I jokingly declared, "You're so weird," followed with "But you're my little weirdo" and a hug. (Note: I do not do this when younger children, who cannot understand the context, are present.)

The grin on her face told me she was tracking perfectly with my gently teasing tone. Even so, we keep even tongue-in-cheek name-calling to a minimum and employ it only in situations where the intent (which is endearment) is crystal clear.

Inevitably, though, we will say something harsh or rude in a moment of temper or even misread a seemingly innocuous interaction, which then leads to hurt feelings. And when this happens, we ask for (and offer) forgiveness.

It's easier for our kids to do this too when we…

Live an Example of Apologizing and Forgiving

Model for your children the art of apologizing and granting forgiveness and require them to participate in the process of doing both. Mamas, I have *such* good news for you. While we never rejoice in our sin or continue in it intentionally so that "grace may abound" (Romans 6:1-2), we *can* glory in the fact that even our transgressions can lead to wonderful teaching moments for our children.

My friend Ginger Hubbard puts it like this in Episode 180 of the *Parenting with Ginger Hubbard* podcast: "When our children see us rightly responding to our own sins in humility, it encourages them to do the same."[2]

I couldn't agree more. If we somehow manage to fake perfection for our children, always hiding our faults or gaslighting our kids into believing *they* are the only ones failing, we will only have succeeded in weaving an elaborate web of lies that leaves our children scrambling for solid footing when, Lord willing, they become parents themselves.

If, however, we take the opportunity provided by our failings to humble ourselves and admit our faults and ask for their forgiveness, we invite our children to celebrate some of the most central truths of the gospel: "All have sinned and fall short" (Romans 3:23), but "by grace you have been saved through faith" (Ephesians 2:8), and we can "be kind to one another, tenderhearted, forgiving one another, as God in Christ forgave you" (Ephesians 4:32).

Many of the questions I receive from moms clearly stem from their hesitancy to see themselves as their children's God-given authority in their homes (I say this with the biblical understanding that husbands and fathers are the spiritual heads of the home but that mothers are often the ones on the front line, establishing and implementing the ground rules). Instead, they second-guess themselves based on what their neighbors are doing, what the latest parenting "expert" on social media is telling them, or even what their own moms are whispering in their ears.

Friends, repentance and forgiveness are both biblical mandates. We have *nothing* to be timid about when it comes to conveying these biblical principles to our children and even compelling them to practice phrases such as "I'm sorry that I ______________" (we name the specific offense committed) and "I forgive you."

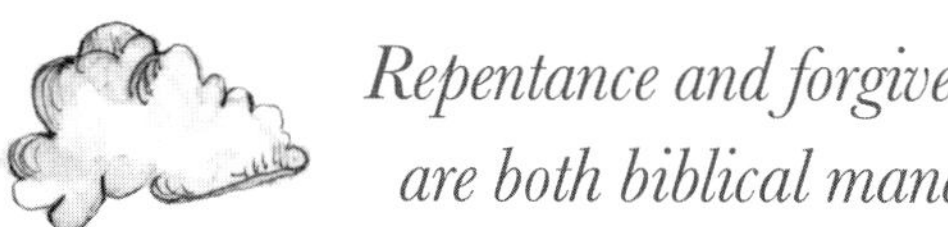

Repentance and forgiveness are both biblical mandates.

The Bible says very little about how we *feel* about forgiveness—merely that "if you forgive others their trespasses, your heavenly Father will also forgive you, but if you do not forgive others their trespasses, neither will your Father forgive your trespasses" (Matthew 6:14-15).

My wise friend Durenda Wilson, a seasoned mom of eight whom you'll hear from at the end of this chapter, adds some wonderful context: "Our emotions can sometimes be helpful indicators, and they are certainly very real, but they cannot be what rules us. We yield everything to God, including our emotions, so apologizing even when they don't feel like it is a good practice."[3]

Be encouraged you are never "too hardcore" simply for holding standards the Bible states as a matter of course. In fact, I encourage you to...

Mute Voices of Discord and Conflict in Your Home

Whether this comes in the form of media that combats your every effort to establish civility in your home (I go into this in depth in chapter 14 of *M Is for Mama*) or even in the form of relatives or neighbors who consistently leave a wake of chaos and bad attitudes behind them, it's your job to exercise appropriate discernment about which influences support your godly goals and which tear them down.

Doing so doesn't necessarily mean we never let our children see foul-mouthed Uncle Rufus or never invite over the neighbor boy who has a hard family life and clearly yearns for the stability and kindness he sees in our home.

It does mean we exercise wisdom in the amount and nature of exposure we allow in such cases.

For our family, this looks like saying no to sleepovers, except for grandparents and one set of cousins. Whenever I share our pretty-much-no-sleepovers policy, I'm always bombarded by two things: (1) demands for reasons why and/or how to deal with explaining your "why" to those who disagree and (2) horror stories from those who agree and have learned about the dangers of sleepovers the hard way.

The answer to demand number one stems from personal experience first (I was exposed at sleepovers as a preteen and teen to most of the junky movies I watched as an otherwise conscientious media consumer; to this day, I wish I'd had more backbone to walk away or speak up since I can't erase certain images from my mind). It also includes knowledge corroborated in those "horror story" messages I mentioned—that no matter how well you think you know the parents of your children's friends, you may not have accounted for hidden sin in one of their lives or in the life of a child you don't know well who may also be attending the sleepover, which could lead to irreparable damage to your precious children. I praise God my only sleepover regrets are objectionable movie scenes and not sexual assault or drug or occult exposure, which is not the case for many I've heard from.

Not only that, but, as we often tell our children, "Nothing you need to do with your friends can't be done before bedtime when adults are awake to keep you safe and enjoy it too."

You may not share our family's conviction in this area, and that is entirely up to *your* family and the Lord, but I give that example as a concrete way of showing what being wise could look like with regard to *how much* access to our children we allow those who hold different standards for righteous behavior.

I could go on with specific suggestions (and I know many of you wish I would, instead of continuing in my exasperating habit of encouraging you to seek God's Word and His Spirit's leading in establishing wise guidelines for *your* family), but I hope you'll hear my heart behind these exhortations: *You*, as the parent, have great agency in your relationship with your children, and this is very good news indeed. Your proactive dedication to pursuing their hearts and teaching them God's ways will often (although not always) lead to a mutual state of like and love between you both.

> ***You****, as the parent, have great agency in your relationship with your children, and this is very good news indeed.*

Struggle 2: Your Children Don't Listen to a Word You Say

Feeling helpless as a parent is one of the most defeating emotions we can ever experience. Whether it's an inability to help your child with a bad habit, an illness, or even a school assignment, those moments when you realize you have neither the knowledge nor the power to "fix it" can twist your insides into knots of anxiety.

But what about the powerless feeling that floods your heart when children stubbornly refuse to heed a word you say? They don't listen when you tell them to stop and look both ways in the parking lot. They don't listen when you instruct them to do their schoolwork. They don't listen when you warn about the dangers of illicit drugs.

They just don't listen.

I know this is far from a hypothetical scenario because I've heard from hundreds of moms who are desperate to feel like all their hard work is paying off but don't believe they're making any headway.

They'll message me asking, "What do you do when your kids hit the defiant stage, the stage where they ignore everything you say, the stage where they're rude, the stage where they act like a complete know-it-all?"

They'll joke (in a pained way) about how their child has never once heeded their instructions and is just one of "those kids" who "has done her own thing from day one" or "is stubborn as all get-out" or "acts like more of a parent than I do."

Both these approaches—stereotyping a childhood stage or stereotyping the child himself—puts the emphasis on the perceived problem rather than turning the question inward and asking, "If my child seems more parental than I do, if my child blows me off, if my child is disrespectful, is there anything I'm consistently doing (or not doing) to contribute to this issue?"

Let me be clear: I am fully aware that children, who are descendants of Adam and inheritors of his sin nature (Romans 5:12), are perfectly capable of choosing wrongly, even if we somehow were to manage to parent perfectly (which we won't, of course). I will address the pitfalls of a fear-based parenting approach, which implies that any faults in our children must always be traced directly to our own doorstep. But for now, let me just say this: It takes great wisdom from the Lord to walk the oh-so-crucial tightrope of accepting responsibility for our part in teaching our children well *without* falling into the trap of believing we will "ruin" our kids every time we make a mistake.

So when I encourage you to examine yourself to see if "there be any grievous way in me" (as King David put it in Psalm 139:24)—to take an honest look at your habits and your motivations to see if there are areas in which you are, perhaps, abdicating a necessary role—it's coming from a place of great compassion, not condemnation.

I *want* you to succeed, and since so much of the parenting advice at our fingertips is neither biblical nor even rooted in Judeo-Christian principles like the Golden Rule or "others before self" (which, yes, come from Scripture), I know how isolating and confusing the conflicting opinions from the world can be.

First, I would encourage you not to pay undue attention to the supposed "stages" that every child will go through. Yes, some developmental benchmarks are predictably common (primal movements, teething, losing said teeth, learning to read, puberty, and so on). But others? It completely depends on the kid.

A mom recently wanted to know what I do when my kids "hit the stage where they insult you." The thing is, thanks to the boundaries we established from an early age in response to the first struggle I addressed, not one of our children has gone through an "insult Mama and Daddy" stage. And I know many other families who can say the same. It doesn't mean our kids never speak disrespectfully to us, because I'll freely admit it can happen. But it does mean I don't subscribe to the idea that, "when your son turns eight, he *will* become a surly jerk who has no respect for you anymore."

And I encourage you to skip this mindset too, both because it won't serve you well even if it does happen and because dreading something that never materializes is a good way to hold our children at arm's length when they need us to draw them close.

Yes, social media can make us feel less alone in a positive way at times, but it can also convince us that everyone is going through homogeneous struggles. To be sure, everyone is fighting a battle, regardless of how private, but it may not be the same as ours, or even as the one a social media influencer shared that received thousands of "Yessss...Ugh, I hate this stage too" responses.

Your preteen daughter may start to distance herself from you as she gains more independence, or she may suddenly trail around after you from room to room, talking nonstop, trying to copy every move you make. Hence why a message asking, "What do you do with the extra-aloof preteen stage?" could just as easily read "extra-clingy" instead. (And each mother would be convinced she's writing about a universal issue, rather than a personal experience.)

The same is true of different personality types. I have one particular child who could easily fall into the stubborn-as-a-mule category if I needed a box for him. Being aware of his tendency toward obstinacy can be helpful. Pigeonholing him? Not so much. Especially since this precious, stubborn boy is also one of our snuggliest and sweetest-natured as well.

What if, instead of trying to pin a lack of connection or poor listening skills on a stage or a natural personality bent, we acknowledged that the Bible exhorts parents to raise their children in the "training and admonition of the Lord" (Ephesians 6:4 NKJV), regardless of what they're "supposed" to be doing at age eleven and three-quarters.

Do we stick our heads in the sand, clueless of common struggles or things our children might be exposed to?

Of course not!

We pay attention, and we look for solutions instead of "me too, and it stinks" fist bumps.

Some practical suggestions if it feels like your kids never listen:

Make Sure You're Being Heard

I know. It's basic. But how many times do we toss a command over our shoulder on our way to the laundry room, holler instructions across the kitchen, or say something to the kids in the back of the van, only to find ourselves fighting annoyance a few minutes later when they act completely clueless about the very thing we just addressed?

Friends, I hate to say this, but we sometimes grow a little lazy in the way we communicate with our kids and, in so doing, set ourselves up for simmering frustration that could be avoided if we'd simply get down on the toddler's level, lift the headphone off our teen's ear, or ask our preteen to face us as we talk.

Sometimes our kids *truly* don't hear us, and when we account for this, instead of simply losing our cool over it, the lines of communication immediately have less static than before.

To be sure, there are also plenty of times your kids hear you but respond with more contrary opinions than cheerful obedience. And when that happens, you must...

Examine Your Guidelines and Rules for Reasonableness

Bedtime is a huge sticking point for many moms, especially as their kids get older. I hear from women every week who feel threatened by their preteens' requests to stay up later, not because they're worried about their child's losing sleep but because they don't want to relinquish their evening "me time."

I get it. It's an adjustment. But I promise you, a knee-jerk "You've gone to bed at 8:00 p.m. your whole life, and I see no need to change now" is not the best response. Chances are, you will need to modify your evening decompression rituals, whether they involve a luxurious bath, an hour of mindless social media scrolling, or getting lost in a historical novel while eating Oreos. Whatever your favorite way to unwind, I truly believe both you and your children will benefit if you are willing to reassess and switch up your routine accordingly.

This doesn't mean you immediately bump bedtime to 10:00 p.m. every night and give up all your de-stressing habits. But it might look like doing an activity together until 8:45 p.m. a couple of times a week and then allowing them to read in bed until 9:00.

The same principles of recalibration could apply to curfews, snack rules, screen time (maybe you need to be stricter!), media content (maybe you need to loosen up?), and so much more.

Perhaps you'll find you've already struck an ideal balance between authority and taking your child's preferences into account. Perhaps you'll find elements that need tweaking.

Either way, by faithfully holding your standards up to the light of Scripture to test their soundness and motivation, you are setting yourself up for the greater likelihood your children will listen to and respect your boundaries.

Since this outcome isn't guaranteed, though, you need to be ready to…

Show Your Children You Really Do Mean What You Say

My kids know when I'm giving distracted instructions, and they will sometimes try to get out of obedience if they think I won't remember what I asked of them. This shouldn't surprise anyone. I know adults who do the same. As convicting as it is to admit, sometimes our kids don't listen to us because we don't sound sincere and we don't seem invested.

So, what does sincere, invested instruction look like? Well, often it looks like picking up toys with the toddler block by painstaking block because they need my physical presence to stay motivated. It looks like being willing to follow through on that promise we dangled in front of our kids' noses as an incentive but then really want to get out of when it comes time to make good on it. In other words, when I tell Theo we can do ten burpees together when he gets done with his math page, I better be ready to throw myself on the floor in a few minutes because homeboy is *motivated* by physical activity. It looks like being willing to put our own phones away when we implement a household "no phones after 7:00 p.m." rule.

Sometimes meaning what we say is as simple as physically walking a child over to the chore we wish for her to complete, giving clear, concise directions, and then staying to watch until she finishes. (And giving a high five or a hug when she does.)

In case you haven't noticed yet, the common denominator behind most of these scenarios is a willingness to inconvenience ourselves for the sake of investing in communicating with our children well.

In case you haven't noticed yet, the common denominator behind most of these scenarios is a willingness to inconvenience ourselves for the sake of investing in communicating with our children well.

The problem is, even if you establish reasonable rules, communicate clearly, and follow through on your instructions, your children will still blow you off sometimes. And when they do, you have to be willing to...

Give Appropriate and Effective Consequences

Often, the offense lends itself to the discipline. Our kids use pennies from the Penny Reward System[4] to "pay" for screen time. One penny equals fifteen minutes of games or shows. They can't start before 3:00 p.m. on a school day or spend more than two pennies in one day. (This does not mean our family never exceeds thirty minutes of screens in a day but that our kids' individual choices top out at half an hour.) They must also monitor their own timers. If they violate any of these well-known, clear family guidelines, they forfeit the right to use pennies for screen time the next day. In other words, a misuse of a privilege results in a curtailing of the same privilege.

Outrage or back talk when we remind them of this consequence extends the ban on screen time for the rest of the week, since we consider media a nonessential, and if love for a nonessential element leads to a struggle to steward the essentials well (namely, treating another person with civility and respect), then that nonessential needs to go for the time being.

Our older kids know showing up after curfew means a "sorry, but no" to the next request for a social activity with their friends at night. Our baking-obsessed twin girls know if they don't heed my instructions to clean up after themselves, they will be given the responsibility of not only a thorough baking-mess cleanup but also a detailed full-kitchen-cabinet wipe down.

You are the parent in your home. You know which consequences will help them remember to make wise choices and which will produce no more than an apathetic shrug from some of your children.

If you're hoping for more lists of infractions and correlating consequences, the fact is, what encourages one child to reassess his behavior won't necessarily do the same for another, nor will a blanket consequence apply to every age. Which means you'll never get an exhaustive catalog of discipline from me, nor do I believe you would benefit from it, since I don't know you or your kids personally.

As always, guiding principles apply, but we can never stop paying attention to the details of the unique ways God has crafted our children's hearts, minds, and souls.

Lest this need for continued vigilance fill you with a sinking sense of failure, may I encourage you that knowing your children well is one of the most worthwhile (and ultimately rewarding) things you will ever do? It is also a role you have been uniquely gifted by God to fill. And, by His grace, you can do it better than anyone else in the world.

A Titus Two Perspective

DURENDA WILSON
author, podcast host, mother of eight

When my husband and I decided to homeschool, little did I know that so much of my time would be spent figuring out how to manage the myriad of relationships in our home. I had made the mistake of believing that my kids would get along most of the time. I was sure they would love each other as much as my husband and I loved them and act accordingly. Instead, at one point, I found myself overwhelmed with the bickering and fighting.

Although we taught our children from a young age to speak respectfully to each other, there came a point when their relationships and disagreements became more complex. Also, as we added more kids to the family, it began to feel as if I was spending most of my time refereeing arguments and getting nowhere. I needed help, but it needed to be clear, simple, and concise, so I went straight to God's Word. What I found in the New Testament, especially, was life-changing. God gives clear directives there to His people on how to treat each other. It made sense to me that the principles God gave to the "family of God" applied to my family as well.

Verses like Romans 12:10 ("Love one another with brotherly affection. Outdo one another in showing honor") and Philippians 2:3 ("Do nothing from selfish ambition or conceit, but in humility count others more significant than yourselves") showed my family and me that we were to work to put each other first in all of our interactions. We needed to honor one another above ourselves.

As parents, this seemed like a daunting task and a huge responsibility, but it was a call to obedience, and we had to trust that as we did the next right thing, encouraging and training our kids to do the same in their relationships, God would bless it. God's Word, not our family's emotions, needed to be our standard.

The word "honor" in the Bible means to "esteem, value, or respect." There is no caveat that we have to "feel" it before we obey. Often obedience requires us to walk by faith, doing what God says first, and eventually, our emotions will follow. Our family worked daily with God's help to apply the principle of honor: our kids honoring each other and us and my husband and I honoring each other and the kids. By the way, when we honor (value our children), we will discipline and train them toward righteousness (Proverbs 13:24 and Hebrews 12:6-11). We noticed that we began to dislike our children most often when we were slacking in this area, so it was a great reminder to get our discipline back on track. None of us honored one another perfectly, but we pressed on, asking for and extending forgiveness and grace when needed.

Moms, I'm now on the other side, and I can tell you that upholding the principle of honor in your home is worth it! Obeying God in this area to the best of our ability has given us a strong, cohesive family that loves each other deeply and is there for one another through thick and thin.

The investment is time-consuming, but it's oh, so worth it!

The Narrative

A WORLDLY RESPONSE TO "WORTH IT"	A BIBLICAL RESPONSE TO "WORTH IT"
Views her children as "the opposition"	Sees her children as the in-progress investment they are
Skips opportunities for training because "it's hard"	Digs in to practical ways to equip her kids with appropriate communication skills and behavior
Avoids self-reflection at all costs	Examines her own motivations and habits for areas of improvement

Action Steps

- Memorize and meditate on Ephesians 6:4: "Do not provoke your children to anger, but bring them up in the discipline and instruction of the Lord."
- Take a moment to write out on sticky notes reminders from this chapter about the inherent worth children have in God's eyes. (Examples: "Children are a blessing." "My kids are image-bearers of God." "Motherhood is a privilege and a godly responsibility." "I get to be my kids' mama.") Post these sticky notes in high-traffic areas (bathroom mirror, fridge, rearview mirror, kitchen sink) as motivation to view your kids with the eyes of Christ.
- Make a list of two areas in which you excel at consistency and two areas that could use some improvement. Pick one problem area to pray about and brainstorm solutions for this week.

Questions

How does viewing children as the "enemy" affect our perspective on motherhood in general and treatment of our children in particular?

Am I allowing influences into my life that perpetuate an attitude of victimhood, abdication of responsibility, or hostility toward my children? If so, which ones?

What are three practical things I can do this week to see my children as blessings and to encourage them to "be a blessing" to their own families and the world?

Prayer

Jesus, You love us, even when we are unlovable and unlikable. Help us to see our children with Your eyes of love and compassion, even when we feel frustrated or stuck. Grant us the wisdom and strength to move forward in Your victory rather than stay mired in defeat. Amen.

CHAPTER 8

The Truth About Honest Motherhood

One evening, just as I was about to climb into bed, I saw an email come through that made my stomach do a flip. I could tell, just by the snatches of phrases I could see, the writer of it was unhappy with me. She had listened to one of my podcast episodes, and she was fed up.

In a podcast series entitled "The Truth About Honest Motherhood," I addressed the online culture of "telling it like it is," which seeks not only to validate but to valorize our struggles as moms. Rather than merely acknowledging the harder aspects of motherhood (which I will never deny) and seeking encouragement or even solutions, the "honest motherhood" movement elevates and amplifies mothering challenges to the point, at times, of entry into a rapidly growing (and seemingly miserable) club.

A quick glance at the thousands of anguished, angry, and affirming comments that roll in on some of the bigger accounts' more popular posts gives some insight into why the claim of "actually telling you the truth about motherhood" (which almost always means highlighting struggles over joys) has become a staple of social media. In short, it "sells."

Not surprisingly, the most common claim to grievance is one we've seen before—that becoming a mom strips us of many (if not all) freedoms and opportunities. I will never deny that motherhood limits our ability to lavish as much time on the same things we did before children. But it does not wipe them out altogether. One particular point I made in this podcast series was that, far from eradicating our abilities to "be anything other than a mother," having children often clarifies and sharpens our interests.

Before motherhood, many of us kept multiple hobby plates spinning and spent much of our time hopping from one activity to the next. Maybe, before children, you crafted maniacally until 1:00 a.m. or chaired three different social clubs or kept a garden and made sourdough *while* volunteering for a local pregnancy resource center. (Of course, maybe you spent too much time scrolling social media, purchasing on impulse, and pinning recipes you never actually made—but let's not talk about that.)

All the productive options I mentioned (and so many more) can be great life choices (assuming you have time to catch up on sleep from all of that late-night crafting). But none of them is likely to emerge completely unscathed from the crucible of compressed time and priorities called "becoming a mother."

And that is perfectly okay.

If there is anything that *should* narrow our scope down to the essentials, it's being in charge of other human beings. If there is any pursuit that *should* take precedence over all others, it's investing in everlasting souls.

*If there is any pursuit that **should** take precedence over all others, it's investing in everlasting souls.*

Not only that, but sometimes the process of becoming "mama" (and the focus and efficiency inherent to doing it well) unlocks an interest or skill previously left untapped—one we might have ignored were our focus not broadened beyond navel-gazing *while* at the same time being skewed closer to home.

Unlocked Potential

A perfect personal example is decorating. As a girl, I much preferred to ride four-wheelers in the mud with a family of seven homeschooled brothers we knew than to hang a solitary poster on my bedroom wall or bother to match my sheets to my bedding.

I simply did not care, nor did I believe myself capable of doing so.

Somehow, to my utter astonishment, being in charge of my own home and bringing children into it unleashed in me a creativity and drive I didn't realize existed. Not only did I *care*, I had *vision*. To be fair, my early vision consisted of painting every room in my house a different color and resulted in what a "friend" called my "country kitchen." But as fifteen years of experience in planning and choosing every detail in two DIY house builds (plus a renovation I'll talk about later) honed my tastes, I began to realize I didn't just love decorating; I was *good* at it. Good enough that people asked to hire me to design their homes as well.

The thing is, I didn't have time to do that. With a steady stream of pregnancy, newborns, and toddlers, it was often a yearslong process to get everything "finished" in my own home (the bare walls in my bathroom still waiting for pictures of my kids are staring daggers at that word), leaving zero time left to invest in anyone else's. Were my children stealing my potential? Were they hindering my ability to exercise my talents?

Yep. They sure were, at least in the application of those talents outside my own home. But my kids were also part of the reason I uncovered that buried talent in the first place. And I was spending my "potential" on our home and on their care and keep, which was the wisest and most impactful use of my talents and time. (Because if I can only "use up" my giftings in one place—especially during the intense years of having only small children—may it be my own home).

Benefitting Motherhoodily

Or take exercise as another example. I've always been an athlete, participating in every sport I could manage: soccer, basketball, softball, volleyball, swimming, tennis, racquetball, pickleball. You name it, I've probably tried it if I could. But it wasn't until I was five months pregnant with Simon that I got certified in group fitness—a *very* good decision that has benefited our family financially (because I am paid to teach classes, and we get a free gym membership to boot) and…*motherhoodily*.

Yes, I just made that word up; I'll explain. When a family benefits *motherhoodily*, it's because Mama finds something that so charges her soul, the effects overflow into every aspect of her life, including parenting and wife-ing, of course.

For some, it's gardening. When you wriggle your fingers down into sun-warmed earth, you can't help but smile. Your mood lifts, and you find yourself regarding your toddler beatifically as he flips soil into the air, instead of resorting to the usual "Stop it! Do you always have to make things so much harder?"

For others, it's reading a really good book. Or painting. Or crocheting. Or giving yourself at-home manicures. It doesn't have to be complicated or expensive. It's your thing. You can manage fine without it, but when you're able to partake, you function better, feel lighter, and act kinder.

I have often said, "I don't have to exercise to be nice, but I am a nicer person when I exercise regularly." It's a whole scientific *thing* (with numerous studies linking exercise endorphins, dopamine, and serotonin levels to better sleep, better sex, more energy, and on and on).

I talk at length in *M Is for Mama* about the Christian view of self-care (which the world calls an essential) versus soul care (which the Bible declares nonnegotiable). Hear me that I am not saying *any* personal interest or beloved hobby can trump the soul-filling benefit of time spent with our heavenly Father. (For that matter, no amount of self-denial in motherhood can substitute for prioritizing God's Word and presence.)

But since it is our gracious Father who designed us to be delighted by the very (good) things that tickle our fancies so, it would be foolish to ignore the way we are designed and completely shut down every other aspect of our beings except the "make food/wipe bums/teach math/correct behavior" categories. To put it another way, when a reader asked me if I struggled with finding my identity in motherhood alone, I said this: "No. Motherhood is my primary vocation and calling. But my life is 'hidden with Christ in God' (Colossians 3:3), and I mother (or do anything else) the way I do because of my identity as a Christ-follower first."

But since it is our gracious Father who designed us to be delighted by the very (good) things that tickle our fancies so, it would be foolish to ignore the way we are designed and completely shut down every other aspect of our beings except the "make food/wipe bums/teach math/correct behavior" categories.

The Mean Side of "It Must Be Nice"

Which brings me back to my disgruntled email friend. As I exhorted my podcast listeners to reject the narrative of diminishment in motherhood and instead look for ways to continue to exercise (or even expand) our God-given talents within the framework of prioritizing our responsibilities to the humans with whom we've been entrusted, this reader responded, "It must be nice to have the capacity to do that. But I can't. I'm barely getting to essentials, and at the end of the day, I have nothing left in the tank. It's sucking me dry, and I hate it."

This frustrated young woman, who has two very small children, proceeded to say she couldn't imagine having to pour herself out like this for the next twenty years without respite.

I understood, at least to some extent. I didn't have the exact struggles she detailed, which she said kept her from completing more than a load of laundry and a haphazard meal each day, but I distinctly remember what it was like to struggle to see beyond the demands of my first two small boys, who were close in age. They needed me for everything from cutting up bites of chicken and clipping their fingernails to bathing and dressing them, buckling their car seats, and so much more.

I'm sure there were times I genuinely believed, like this young woman, that I would still be doing these things for them when they were eighteen years old. (And we're not the only ones, as evidenced by the fact that I get asked multiple times every week how I manage to clip ten children's fingernails—a query which makes me giggle every time I watch my hulking teenage boys walk by).

Even so, I would like to submit to you, dear readers, that "must be nice"—and its close cousin "it sure would be nice if"—are two of the most joy-stealing combinations of words on the planet.

Allow me to present you with two very different perspectives on the same scenario to illustrate this claim.

In response to my sharing videos and pictures from our anniversary trip to Scotland on social media, one reader sent me a message that said the following: "Thank you so much for taking the time to share your trip with us. My husband and I have always wanted to go to Scotland, but we don't have the financial ability to do so right now. It's so fun to get to experience it through your account. What a gift!"

Even so, I would like to submit to you, dear readers, that "must be nice"—and its close cousin "it sure would be nice if"—are two of the most joy-stealing combinations of words on the planet.

I responded by commending her for having such a gracious attitude of contentment and encouragement. It's rare to find, especially on the internet, and even in our own hearts at times.

The second interaction began with a "must be nice" comment on a video I posted, and it ended with a personal message urging me to "read the room; no one wants to hear about your trip to Scotland when we're all having to choose between making mortgage payments and buying food." The parting shot? "You represent Christ. Do better."

I didn't respond to that one because doing so didn't feel productive. But the contrast was so marked it got me mulling over the ways I can have a version of the second response even when I know for a fact the Bible calls me to have the first.

After all, 1 Timothy 6:6-8 says, "But godliness with contentment is great gain, for we brought nothing into the world, and we cannot take anything out of the world. But if we have food and clothing, with these we will be content."

Notice it doesn't say if we have kids who just stay healthy for at least three months at a time, with this we will be content.

Or if we can have as nice of a family vehicle as the neighbors, with this we will be content.

Or even, if our children obey us the first time instead of requiring us to put down the nursing baby, get up, and cross the room to kneel down beside them at eye level and engage, with *this* we will be content.

I've never sent a resentful message to a stranger about her anniversary trip. And I don't claim to fully know or comprehend this woman's particular struggles, because they are different from my own. But I will admit the phrase "must be nice" has trailed through my mind when my husband walks to his office and closes the door to sit down at his computer and work uninterrupted for hours at a time. Meanwhile, I wrangle two fractious toddlers while teaching fractions, painfully aware of the fact I have a writing deadline looming for which no office hours exist. A ghost of "it sure would be nice" has skittered through my thoughts when I walk into the perfectly organized home of a friend whose children seem so much more on top of keeping their rooms clean than mine do. A version of "wouldn't that be nice" can bubble to the surface of my consciousness when I see a mom "bouncing back" to her pre-baby jeans within a month, while certain portions of my post-forty body seem to have bounced their last bounce two pregnancies ago.

I'll tell you the truth, though. I've been the recipient of too many "must be nice" comments courtesy of the internet and have read too much of God's Word to believe for longer than two seconds rubbed together that dwelling on all the ways our life "sure would be nicer if we ______________" leads to anything other than what Hebrews 12:15 describes as a "root of bitterness" that "springs up and causes trouble."

Rejoicing with Those Who Rejoice

A friend shared with me the following verse, which I had never fully considered before she explained what she learned by doing a deep dive into it as a way of combating envy and discontentment.

It reads like this: "Remember me, Lord, in *Your* favor toward your people. Visit me with Your salvation, so that I may see the prosperity of Your chosen ones, that I may rejoice in the joy of Your nation, that I may boast with Your inheritance" (Psalm 106:4-5 nasb).

If you're having trouble connecting the dots between "boasting with Your inheritance" and avoiding a "must be nice" mindset, let me break it down for you like she did for me.

That first verse is a cry for the Lord to "remember me" when He shows favor to His "chosen ones" (which would be all believers)—not so He'll show us the same exact flavor of favor but so we'll be granted the ability to "rejoice in the joy of Your nation." In other words, this is David's way of asking God to check his jealous heart and replace it instead with one that can "rejoice with those who rejoice" (Romans 12:15).

Or, as my friend put it, "When our brothers and sisters in Christ are doing well, it takes *nothing* away from us, unless we let it diminish our joy. It should be a *net positive* when members of the body of Christ prosper, whatever that looks like. I should not want less for you, even if I don't have the advantages I crave. It's not a zero-sum game."

Anybody else feel her conscience cruelly pricked by this simple yet profoundly difficult-to-live-out truth? Mine was smarting for sure.

That's okay, though. As Puritan preacher Thomas Watson put it, "That prayer is most likely to pierce heaven which first pierces one's own heart."[1]

A Net Positive for the Whole Family

This idea of being excited when others prosper naturally includes our children. Rather than resenting the care they require, what if we saw the way they thrive when we pour energy into them as a net positive for our whole family? What if we asked the Lord to help us "rejoice in their gladness" rather than grind our teeth at their neediness?

My friend Allison, from the Instagram account Her Heart's Home, described the shift in her heart attitude from one of resentment at years of waking early to creep from the room with a wide-awake infant while everyone else sleeps in during a family vacation to one of being thankful for a special time of bonding (with her baby and the Lord). "There I was on a trip, and I'm sleeping less, relaxing less, and grasping at my idea of what it would 'ideally' look like. I've learned to take those thoughts captive. I've learned that that mindset only stole my joy.

Though still not always easy, I'm thankful that time has helped me adjust my expectations and perspective. I'm thankful that I didn't let those early years deter us from enjoying trips and adventures. I'm thankful for the memories."

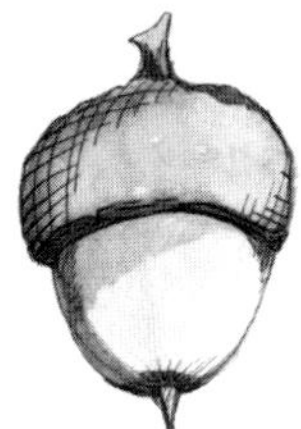

What if we asked the Lord to help us "rejoice in their gladness" rather than grind our teeth at their neediness?

Notice Allison doesn't ignore or invalidate the struggle. Instead, she acknowledges the challenge but then presses through it toward gratitude. Could she have stayed mired in that feeling of "it sure would be nice if the baby would sleep in"? Absolutely. But such a mindset wouldn't have served her, and it's not serving you either, friends.

"Must be nice" may be a staple of "honest motherhood" in the sense that it's truly how we feel at times, but it's also hardly the whole story.

Sometimes, when I'm on my knees, scrubbing the mildew that stubbornly creeps into the corners of my shower tiles, and "it sure would be nice to have more help with the house" crosses my mind, I remember that I used to have outside cleaning help when the twinsies were small. And while it *was* nice, it was also stressful to keep up with which day someone was coming to clean, remember to clear all the "we live here" mess out of her way, and keep the kids focused on schoolwork at the kitchen island so they wouldn't undo her handiwork milliseconds after she completed it. To be honest, I was relieved when we made the decision to focus on tackling the housework as a family again.

In that moment of candor, I feel thankful for the pace at which I'm able to address cleaning projects, and I praise God for granting me the privilege of investing so many years in children who are now able to accomplish household tasks alongside me.

False "honesty" in motherhood assures you that any mom who seems consistently joyful is either faking it or has some upper hand you've been denied. It insists the only way to tell the truth is to get down in the mud of mothering, feel around for the slimiest and grimiest struggles, and hold them high as trophies of authenticity. It focuses primarily on our lack and on the fantasy of the contentment we are sure to feel if only we could trade places with the girl who has "a village."

Truly honest motherhood understands that genuine contentment isn't tied to circumstances. Some days will feel achingly hard, and we can take them to the Lord, completely depleted, and be granted new mercies for the morning. Some days will zip by in a blur of happy memories, and we can take them to the Lord in praise. Some days will be utterly mundane, and we can take them to the Lord for purpose. All days are worth the effort because we have been granted this work at this time with these humans as a way of serving and loving God and His people well.

Truly honest motherhood understands that genuine contentment isn't tied to circumstances. Some days will feel achingly hard, and we can take them to the Lord, completely depleted, and be granted new mercies for the morning.

A Titus Two Perspective

ANGIE TOLPIN

author, podcast host, cofounder of
Be Courageous Ministries, mom of nine

Our bodies are magnificent, created with a remarkable ability to partner with God in bringing forth life. And while this experience of pregnancy is different for everyone, one thing we can all agree on is that it grew us. Just as the stretch marks or other scars on our bodies from the journey toward motherhood reflect physical growth or tell some of the story of the experience we had, they truly represent a deeper growth that has forever changed us. This growth isn't just encapsulated in the physical changes in our bodies, yet these stretch marks symbolize the emotional, mental, and spiritual growth from each challenge a woman faces.

As the years go on and you continue your journey of motherhood, you've likely experienced many growth spurts—from learning not to be too controlling and to let your child fall down and get back up again on their own, to letting them make mistakes, to trusting them behind the wheel as they learn to drive, and everything in between. Each experience we have in our mothering journey helps equip and prepare us for what is to come. In *Redeeming Childbirth*, I call pregnancy "God's Motherhood Bootcamp." Just as those sleepless nights during pregnancy prepare a mama for night feedings with her newborn, so each milestone we reach helps prepare us for the next challenge we meet in this life.

When I mentor younger moms, they often ask how I do all I do: homeschooling, homesteading, business and ministry with my husband, and managing my home. My response is that I didn't do it all at once. Just like any older mom you might question, my life is a reflection of God's grace over many years, patiently leading me and teaching me. When I didn't listen, He disciplined and rebuked me. He walked me through really hard times, and I spent countless hours seeking the Lord, asking Him what He had to teach me, and how I could best glorify Him as I walked through the hard junk we face in this life. I learned and grew over time. Each time a new baby came to our family or even when I wrote my first book, which was a labor of love, obstacles were met and my capacity grew. Sometimes it was painful; other times, not so much.

Kind of like pregnancy, there are moments when the growth of your baby hurts. And the truth is, it's the same as they get older. There will be times when you may feel unprepared, and you'll experience growth pains in your relationships—but those experiences are meant to draw you more towards the heart of the Father, seeking His wisdom, and leaning into the truth found in His Word. My exhortation to you would be to submit to the refining work of the Holy Spirit and the sanctification that leads to growth.

First Timothy 2:15 says, "Yet she will be saved through childbearing—if they continue in faith and love and holiness, with self-control." The "saved" in this verse is referring to an aspect of ongoing sanctification that takes place throughout one's life, which is why we see the text say "if," exhorting us to continue our journey of motherhood in faith, love, and holiness, with self-control. These four attributes are a choice we must continually pursue, but we need the Holy Spirit to help us. May we all be women of the Word who seek to live our lives in a way that brings glory to God the Father and our Lord Jesus Christ.

After all, this journey of motherhood is not only about being a shepherd in our child's life to help them grow up to know the Lord and love Him but also growing up ourselves—keeping a teachable, humble heart and recognizing that we always have room to grow.

Remember, those stretch marks are something to be cherished—they represent the growth God has done in your life and the promise that He will continue to grow you and build your capacity for more.

The Narrative

A WORLDLY RESPONSE TO "WORTH IT"	A BIBLICAL RESPONSE TO "WORTH IT"
Conflates "honesty" with airing all grievances	Acknowledges both hard things and enjoyable things
Employs "must be nice" whenever her reality doesn't match what she wishes it were	Knows that parenting with an eye on what someone else has only ever produces resentment
Searches for validation of struggle	Seeks solutions and wisdom

Action Steps

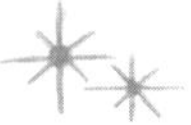

- Memorize and meditate on 1 Timothy 6:6-8: "But godliness with contentment is great gain, for we brought nothing into the world, and we cannot take anything out of the world. But if we have food and clothing, with these we will be content."
- Make a list of three things about which you often think, "It must be nice." Then make a list of three things about which you can honestly say, "It is so nice."
- Start each day with a prayer of gratitude for one of your "it is so nice" categories. Make a goal of adding two more "it is so nice" statements by the end of the week.

Questions

Do you follow any accounts that claim to be telling the truth about motherhood but in reality seem to equate honesty with negativity and commiseration? If so, what benefit do you receive from them?

How can a "must be nice" attitude keep you from appreciating what you do have?

What do you think "honesty" in motherhood from a worldly perspective conveys to your husband, your children, your friends, and your community?

Prayer

Lord, You have given us everything we need for life and godliness in Your Word. And You supply all of our needs according to Your riches in Christ Jesus. May we have eyes to see Your goodness and hearts of contentment to dwell in it. Amen.

CHAPTER 9

Enough Because God Made You So

"How do you spend enough time with each child? I don't think I do, and I only have two kids."

"Do you feel like you're giving each child what he needs? I worry about this constantly."

"Do you think of your children as individuals or just kind of a blob?"

These questions, along with endless similar variations, land in my WWKW inbox every single week. And while I think they convey some common misconceptions about larger-than-average families, the primary underlying motivation seems to be a gnawing worry about not being "enough."

I've already shared my bedrock beliefs on this topic (you aren't enough—Jesus is, and that's better), but beyond the principles of our heavenly Father's omnipotence (which can help us breathe more easily in the knowledge we were never the ones in control anyway), the parallel truth is that we are exactly enough for our children because God, in His sovereignty, has equipped us to be just that in just the moment we need to be.

Mothers seem to be increasingly primarily concerned not with meeting their children's needs but with exceeding them. Whether or not they realize it, they don't want to be enough. They want to be *more than.*

Yes, there are plenty of women in the world who aren't providing for their children's basic needs, but these are not the mothers messaging me most of the time. The ones I hear from are feeding their children, buying them clothes, doing their laundry, taking them to soccer practice, bandaging their boo-boos, reading them bedtime stories, and hosting birthday parties.

And they *still* don't feel adequate.

Why?

Well, if this is you, perhaps the niggling sensation of deficiency in the back of your mind stems from harsh criticism you received from your own mother, aunt, or third-grade teacher. Words have power, and unless we are faithful to preach the truth of God's Word to our own hearts daily, it's easy to constantly chase an elusive sense of accomplishment, especially if it feels like someone else is dangling it just beyond our reach.

Or maybe you've swallowed the social media myth of "perfect motherhood." You regularly consume images of coordinating sibling outfits, impossibly smooth foreheads and shiny hair, over-the-top party décor, and elaborate meal prep, and you begin to believe, if your children aren't getting *that* mom, they're missing out.

There's also the distinct possibility that you're experiencing genuine twinges of conscience as you recognize the fact that so much time spent escaping to a fantasy world on social media—even one you find yourself resenting—has caused you to miss out on opportunities to invest more deeply in your children at home.

Because isn't that typical of how Satan operates? Luring us away from our primary responsibilities, causing us to question, begrudge, or forsake our parenting duties, then whispering in our ear, "You're going to mess them up anyway, so you might as well give up now" when we try to free ourselves from the vice grip of comparison and distraction?

The insidious lie that nothing we do is going to have much effect or ever measure up can creep into even the most confident mom's heart, but here's the truth:

Somehow, in the extraordinary math of motherhood, 1:1 is a perfectly wonderful ratio, and you are enough for that one child because God has made you enough. But so is 1:2, 1:3, 1:7, 1:10, and so on. Sure, the logistics can get more complicated the more children you have. The efforts will intensify. The focus must sharpen. But just like Jesus did with the feeding of the 5,000 in Matthew, He is able to multiply our meager efforts, concentration, resolve, energy, and resources the moment we throw up our hands and declare with the disciples, "Send the crowds away to go into the villages and buy food for themselves."

He is able to multiply our meager efforts, concentration, resolve, energy, and resources the moment we throw up our hands.

I started out simply using this verse as an example, but as I read it again, it sounds like something a mother might legitimately tell the Lord. "Oh, Jesus. I fed these folks three square meals yesterday, plus 562 snacks. And I fed them breakfast this morning. And now they have the nerve to want to eat *again*! Please send these people somewhere else for sustenance. I'm tapped out."

And what does the Lord reply? Not "You're right. It's too much. You should go have a spa day." But instead "You give them something to eat."

Shoot. That wasn't what we (or the disciples) were hoping for. As our shoulders slump and we sigh, "But, Lord, I only got five hours of sleep last night and have only had two short showers all week," Jesus looks at us with compassion and says, "Bring me what you've got." (This whole story can be found in Matthew 14:13-21, in case you're wondering.)

And then He takes our lack and our exhaustion and our self-pity and somehow turns them into something that satisfies both us and our children. We might even find ourselves with some leftovers like the disciples did with their twelve baskets of fish and bread, the miraculous overflow of only five loaves and two fish to begin with.

More often than not, though, we end the day with all our resources completely used up, miraculously sufficient, with nary a drop to spare.

Not only that, but when we become convinced a situation is too hard and too much to bear, God often broadens the scope of our understanding of "too much" by giving us even more to handle and a compensatory measure of His grace to match.

Jennifer Flanders, my mentor, dear friend, and voluntary first editor of these very pages you're reading, will share with you at the end of this chapter how the Lord took her from fearing her own inadequacy when bringing home her first newborn (of twelve!) to complete reliance on Him when her worst fears were almost realized with her firstborn's type 1 diabetes diagnosis.

I'll let her share the details; just know her story of learning to flex motherhood muscles made strong and sinuous by pressure and trial is one many of us will relate to. When we cry out to God for help, rather than spending our time second-guessing ourselves (or others), we can be assured He will answer (even if His response is different than we'd hoped).

And that, my friends, is why, whenever that niggling voice of doubt begins to hiss condemnation in my ear, I am able to ask God for wisdom in how to discern "mom guilt" from true Holy Spirit conviction (I have an entire chapter on this in *M Is for Mama*) and to return again to my job of being the greatest living expert on *The Halberstadt Children*, with the help of three trusty principles: careful observation, intentionality, and connection.

All three of these guideposts have served me well for almost twenty years of parenting in keeping the "Am I doing enough?" voices at bay. They bolster my confidence that, even if my efforts fall short by some worldly standard, as long as my goal is to honor God with my actions, words, and heart posture, it will always be sufficient in His sight.

So let's unpack what these three principles look like on a practical level.

AS LONG AS MY GOAL IS TO HONOR GOD WITH
MY ACTIONS, WORDS, AND HEART POSTURE,
IT WILL ALWAYS BE SUFFICIENT IN HIS SIGHT.

Careful Observation

Contrary to what some of the questions I receive about large families imply, in my experience, moms of many know their children inside out, backward, and sideways. So do moms of one, two, or four. Why? Because we're all over here greedily memorizing the details that make our kids tick the way they do, lick their spoons the way they do, say "ick" about the foods they do.

I listen to my friend Beverly (who has six children) meticulously list the classes her middle daughter is taking in her freshman year at college while also waxing eloquent about the craft kick her teenage daughter is on at home. Meanwhile, my friend Courtney, who has a young boy and girl close in age, describes her daughter, whom she calls "spicy," in contrast to her slow and steady son. She clearly delights in both personalities and is well versed in their nuances. And my friend Kim, who has eleven children, including a special-needs toddler perched on her lap, pours her heart out about her hopes for her oldest daughter's romance with a promising young man, followed by astute observations about her rambunctious middle-school boys.

When we practice the mundane but oh-so-important art of paying attention, we are rewarded with concrete, actionable ways to love our children well (a desire at the root of so many of the anxious questions I receive).

Have a child who loves to dance? Me too! Several, actually. Although my second son, Simon, is the most rhythmic of the bunch and can pick up most physical movements with ease.

Another child loves to bake? I have two of those! My twin girls are baking fanatics who would happily make brownies *and* muffins *and* cookies, all in one day. Come to think of it, they sometimes do (it's a wonder we don't all have triple chins). I love this about them, and not just because I get to eat the fruits (usually baked into pies) of their culinary labors.

Got any tactile learners? My ten-year-old son, Theo, is into all things engineering and has been known to create impressively symmetrical and sturdy designs out of simple wooden slats, not to mention turning a cleaning brush into a quirky mobile creation called Scrubbie, thanks to a circuit kit, a battery, and some glue-on googly eyes.

I could give you more examples as evidence I view my children as individuals rather than a "herd," but I doubt any mom of any number truly needs convincing if only she will search her own extensive database of "kid facts," which surely occupies a solid 80 percent of her available gray matter hard drive.

If noticing were an Olympic sport, we mamas would dominate first, second, and third place on the medals podium. It's built into our motherhood DNA, and we would do well to embrace that, because doing so is the first step toward being able to tell the devil to take a hike the next time he tries to convince you you're a parenting flop.

Intentionality

So we know all this *stuff* about our kids. Now what?

Now we very intentionally assimilate that knowledge and do something about it.

Take Simon's love for dance. When I noticed his natural ability to groove, I started thinking of wholesome ways to cultivate that. Soon, I landed on YouTube tutorials for a fun, athletic dance style called shuffling. One day, as a family, we spent a fun, sweaty hour and a half learning the most basic shuffle step ever—the running man. Were we good? No, we were not. Did we look coordinated? Girl, please. But did we have fun? *You bet your stretch marks!*

Pretty soon, Simon and I advanced beyond the most basic steps, and I found myself scrambling to stay ahead of his skills while researching clean music and new shuffle dance steps for us to learn.

A bit of intentionality with a smidge of effort turned into a unique way to bond. Win!

Or take the twinsies' baking obsession. It started five years ago when I had just birthed Titus and Toby. They came to me with the idea to make breakfast for our family every Saturday morning, and, if I'm honest, my first thought was "NO, THANK YOU!" I knew how much havoc two eight-year-olds could wreak in the kitchen. Plus, Saturday mornings were a rare opportunity to go back to bed for an hour or two after a particularly challenging night of nursing two babies on repeat.

It took every bit of my willpower and some powerful nudging from the Holy Spirit for me to reluctantly say yes to their scheme.

Many of my concerns proved valid. The messes were plentiful. The sleep was scarce. The way my blood pressure spiked every time they burned entire batches of treats was real.

But bit by bit, thanks to the Lord's helping me beat back that desire for easier Saturday mornings, my girls have become more than proficient bakers and genuine helps to me when I make dinner. (Nola's big fluffy dinner rolls are the perfect complement to any meal.)

When we were forced by a house flood to renovate our entire kitchen, I was able to very intentionally plan every detail of a baking corner in our new design with Evy and Nola in mind. Being able to exercise that kind of intentionality in such a specific way brought me so much joy as a mama, and the space continues to thrill the twinsies too.

In a full-circle moment of triumph I could never have anticipated, my publisher, Heather, who knows all about the baking adventures in our home, offered Evy and Nola a cookbook deal. Friends, we never know the end result of our perseverance until we get there. Sometimes it's not until glory. Sometimes it materializes in a sweet tween baking book called *Double Delights* (coming soon).

Being intentional to foster Theo's interest in engineering meant a Christmas present of a three-month subscription to a project-in-a-box that ended up extending well into the rest of the year due to his utter delight in the process of assembling each month's kit. The most important part is making sure to openly admire his creations upon completion.

Noticing Della's love of writing looks like saying, "Yep, wanna bring your laptop to write too?" when she asks me if I'm heading into town to work on a manuscript. The twinbies need regular snuggles throughout the day, so prioritizing that means taking a fifteen-minute break from dishes or laundry or emails to pile on the couch with a stack of books and a small body tucked under each arm. Shiloh's obsession with the great outdoors often leads to his plopping down in my lap and requesting that we search my phone for identifications of the various caterpillars, frogs, lizards, and moths he's forever bringing into the house. I've already mentioned Ezra's love language (pickleball and food, obviously). And Honor will always beg for another chapter of *Hank the Cow Dog*.

These examples certainly aren't the only ways I practice intentionality with my children. It's a constant, ever-changing flow of noticing and then acting. And then recalibrating on the days I've failed at both. None of it would make for a splashy social media video or be of much interest to anyone but me and the child involved. And that, my friends, is how it should be. A steady drip, drip, drip of everyday choices that fill our children's hearts to overflowing.

Sadly, so many moms have allowed the world to convince them that, if they are not systematically doing one-on-one dates with their children, if they are not regaling them with pony rides and ice cream and trips to the mall, if they are not having compelling conversations over meals in their favorite restaurants, they can't possibly hope to truly know their children well.

There's nothing inherently wrong with any of these things (and many things right!), but to quote my friend Jennifer, "If we're not careful, our mother love can morph into smother love." Extravagant, bespoke outings simply aren't necessary for strong parent-child bonds and can create unrealistic expectations in the hearts of our kids when they would otherwise have been perfectly content with a less flashy option.

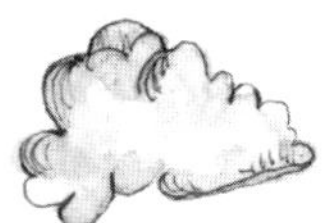

Extravagant, bespoke outings simply aren't necessary for strong parent-child bonds.

Many of the best one-on-one chats I have with my kids take place on strolls through the grocery store after I've said, "Sure you can come, but you'd better grab your shoes quickly before anyone else notices," and then we sneak away for thirty minutes to an unglamorous destination made special nonetheless by the company we keep. The same goes for washing dishes elbow to elbow as we belt out Shane & Shane ballads together, walking hand in hand down our long driveway to check the mail at twilight, or going to an early class at the gym, just the two of us. In other words, each seemingly insignificant little square of mundane time becomes a beautiful quilt of intentionality and shared history when stitched together over the course of years.

Each seemingly insignificant little square of mundane time becomes a beautiful quilt of intentionality and shared history when stitched together over the course of years.

Some of the sweetest memories for our entire family involve *all* of us gathered around the kitchen island, eating dinner, telling stories, and laughing over shared experiences. The three nights our older kids, Shaun, and I walked to a pub called The Water Rats on the corner of our rental's street in London to drink sparkling lemonade, slurp spoonfuls of silky lemon posset, and talk about our favorite memories from our European adventure will forever be emblazoned on my brain in happy remembrance.

Being intentional to foster a collective culture (as opposed to only prioritizing one-on-one relationships) is so important to creating the kind of dynamic that makes our kids *want* to come home for the holidays. I'll dive more into the particulars of this in the next chapter, but I wanted to share a longtime reader's thoughts in response to a WWKW question that went like this: "How do you make sure you have deep relationships with your children, especially when there are 'so many'?"

My reader (who has six kids) sent me this reply: "This question always puzzles me. Because who says that deep relationships are *only* formed through one-on-one interactions. There is so much depth in doing things together as a family! Playing games together, studying the Word together, just talking and hanging out. I honestly feel relational depth is enhanced by having more kids. But I may be biased."

She makes some really good points—namely, that we need to be careful not to let culture define "deep relationship" for us when we can clearly see the fruit of the efforts we are being intentional to make, regardless of whether they match someone else's ideal. (And this includes the mom of "only" one who is now wondering whether her child can achieve depth in his relationships without the benefit of multiple siblings. Good news! He can!)

Certainly, part of being intentional is noticing when a child does seem disconnected, isn't feeling seen or heard, and does need either more individual attention or more conscious inclusion into the group.

Our family does something called Bible Buzzers—a trivia game we created to quiz our kids on information from our specific family Bible readings—on Sunday evenings. It's a group activity, but it lends itself more toward older kid participation. Even so, Shaun is careful to include questions for the younger children. They won't always get the more detailed queries, but they know an age-appropriate question reserved just for them is coming, and they get so excited when it does!

Connection

So you've put in the work of noticing, and you've been intentional to invest, but to what end?

The answer is connection.

Saying yes to our children's requests to accompany us to the grocery store is all well and good until we zone out and drag them through our errands at speed, responding to their chatter with monosyllabic grunts and annoyance (sure, it happens; but it's not the goal).

Unfortunately, even the most selfless gestures become rote when we lose sight of the purpose behind them. It's possible to be intentional enough to take your daughter to breakfast because you know it's her favorite meal of the day, only to spend the majority of the time on your phone, taking calls that could have waited or checking "one more email real quick."

Or how about the times I've sat down to give my six-year-old my undivided attention, only to glaze over a minute into his endless "spider facts" and answer with a startled "Huh?" when he asks me which arachnid, of the three he's just described, is my favorite. Again, such occurrences are common, and there is grace for imperfectly executed efforts to connect too. But what a delight to the souls of even our smallest and most verbose kiddos when we can say with enthusiasm, "Oh, the banana spider, for sure. He's just so cool!"

To that end, may I suggest a few steps toward growing a genuine connection with each of your children?

Stay Off Your Phone

Nothing says, "I'm only pretend listening" like frequently glancing at our screens in the middle of a conversation with another human. (And I know this because I've both done it and been on the receiving end.)

If your phone seems to possess overwhelming allure, physically setting it face down in a place where you can't easily grab it (perhaps attached to a charging cable in another room?) is one of the most foolproof ways to recognize that God really will "provide the way of escape, that you may be able to endure [temptation]" (1 Corinthians 10:13).

Make Lists of Things to Talk About

It may seem wooden or disingenuous, but I've heard from enough mamas who ask me for specific ways to connect—especially with their teen boys—that I know simple conversation is a legitimate struggle.

The morning before I wrote these words, I had an early appointment. As I backed my van out of the garage, I noticed Simon shooting hoops in the relative cool of what would soon be a blistering July day. The idea of inviting him to come with me to my appointment and then grab breakfast crossed my mind, but I almost dismissed it (he dearly loves his basketball drills). Instead, I poked my head out the window and said, "Wanna come?" With a grin, he said, "Sure! Let me put on some deodorant!" (Considerate, no?)

I don't keep a physical list of topics for Simon, but I certainly have a running mental tab, which goes like this:

Basketball
Sports therapy
Fitness
Music
Food
Friends

And, indeed, we addressed each of these categories at length, ending with a discussion about the greatest male and female singers of all time (and what true greatness actually means).

Ask Questions

It's so easy, as mamas, to do all the talking. I am especially guilty of filling awkward gaps with stories or jokes. But one of the best ways to connect with our kids is to ask questions and then allow them the time and space to answer. Yes, depending on your child's personality, you may need to prompt or ask follow-up questions to further lubricate the conversation's flow.

But, as with so many other habits, the more we practice, the more adept we become in knowing which questions to ask and then in exercising patience as we await the answers.

Do the Things They Love

Sure, connecting with some of our children is easy because we share interests or personality traits. And there is so much benefit to inviting our children into the tasks and passions that already hold our attention so they can participate in some way. But recognizing our kids as unique beings who reflect the *imago Dei* in distinct and wonderful ways means learning to prioritize their preferences at times, even when it's not our thing.

Once, on Instagram, I shared a story of riding a roller coaster at a theme park with my older children as an encouragement to my readers to step outside our comfort zones for the sake of connection. I had volunteered to stay with the little ones for the majority of the day, concerned with the mild vertigo that riding roller coasters has caused me as I've gotten older. But on the last ride of the day, I decided to chance it, feeling pretty sure I'd be fine. Thankfully, I was right! The ride was a blast. I didn't get dizzy. And Ezra, Simon, and Della loved that I jumped in at the last minute.

I concluded by saying that, although roller coasters might not be a worthwhile gamble for every mom (and should certainly be avoided if any real danger were present), we are equipped to discern the "roller coasters" we say yes to that will impact our relationships with our specific children the most.

The overwhelming majority of responses were positive (including multiple private messages from mamas telling me this post was just what they needed to hear), but despite the caveats, I still received several indignant comments about "promoting unsafe practices" or "ignoring our own needs to pander to our kids."

Just when I felt myself becoming disheartened by some commenters' seemingly willful determination to miss the point of the story, I received the following welcome encouragement (paraphrased here for the sake of brevity):

The point of your post was perfectly clear, and it was a nudge from the Lord. I'm a plus-size mama who was spending my time at a water park on my phone as my children went down the slides. I'm not in the best shape, and climbing all those stairs intimidated me. Not only that, but you have to weigh yourself at the top of the ride. As I read your post, I felt the deepest conviction that I was spending time with strangers on the internet instead of making memories with my children. I put my phone down, climbed those stairs, stood on that scale, and rode those slides multiple times with my kids.

This last part is verbatim: "My kids loved it...My legs were jelly, my lungs burned, but I set an example for my daughter and son and made memories. Thank you for sharing so God can use you in the lives of others."

I don't know that I've ever before cheered out loud upon receiving a message from a reader, but I did that day. And I had tears streaming down my face as I ran to read it to Shaun in his office. What a beautiful example of choosing to do something you don't love for the sake of connection with someone you do! And what an incredible opportunity to support and encourage another mama (and receive multiplied encouragement in return!).

Pray Specifically for Each Child

Taking the time to mention each child to the Lord by name and ask for His help in connecting with their hearts is so crucial, yet often overlooked. The Lord is never too busy to hear about even the most seemingly insignificant struggles or victories. And the good news is we can do this at any point throughout our day, not just in some slippery ideal of a quiet time that never seems to materialize.

As you carpool, pray for your son's "rage monster" struggles.

As you meal prep, ask the Lord to give you patience with that one child who never stops talking.

As you flip a load of laundry from the washer to the dryer, commit your daughter's tendency toward anxiety to the One who gives peace that passes all understanding (Philippians 4:7).

Remember, our heavenly Father cares about the sparrows and the grass of the field (Matthew 6:25-30). How much more does He care for your precious children?

I know for a fact there is at least one mom reading these words and thinking, "I really have messed it up. It's too late. I can't start any of this now. My bad habits are too ingrained."

I know this because countless moms have confided having such thoughts to me. I want to encourage you that the devil (whose name comes from the Greek *diabolos*, which translates as "slanderer" or "accuser") would love nothing better than for you to believe your past failures must inform your future efforts.

I want to encourage you that the devil (whose name comes from the Greek **diabolos**, *which translates as "slanderer" or "accuser") would love nothing better than for you to believe your past failures must inform your future efforts.*

The antidote to his allegations also comes from the book of Matthew: "But seek first the kingdom of God and his righteousness, and all these things will be added to you" (Matthew 6:33).

In other words, start *today*. Take baby steps. Set your face like flint toward the goal of renewed purpose and right priorities. Ask the Lord for wisdom. He will give it.

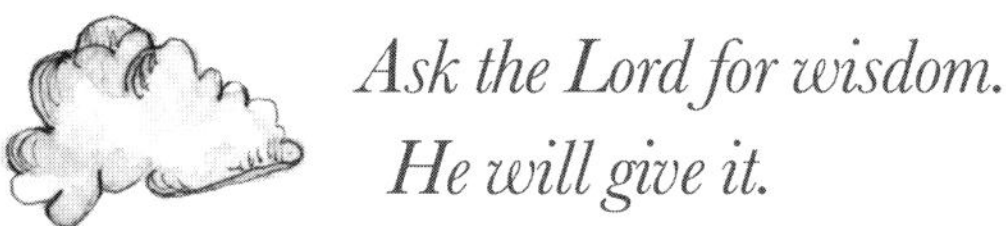

Ask the Lord for wisdom. He will give it.

"Therefore do not be anxious about tomorrow, for tomorrow will be anxious for itself. Sufficient for the day is its own trouble" (Matthew 6:34).

Thankfully, the good news is that sufficient for the day is its own joy, as well, because "the joy of the LORD is your strength" (Nehemiah 8:10). I am fully convinced the investment of time, attention, and care inherent to each of the steps I've described in this chapter is one of the most worthwhile and joy-filled pursuits we will ever undertake as human beings.

What a privilege to know, love, and disciple another eternal soul like it's our job. Because it is.

A Titus Two Perspective

JENNIFER FLANDERS

author, editor, podcast host, mother of twelve

A twinge of uncertainty swept over me when—two days after pushing my firstborn into the world (he weighed ten pounds, six ounces and crowned far too quickly for an epidural)—it came time to bring baby home from the hospital.

"What have I gotten myself into?"

The nurse made my head swim with rapid-fire directives on breastfeeding, burping, bathing, diapering, and swaddling my baby. She also demonstrated the proper way to position him for sleep: "Always on his tummy! Never on his back!"—exactly opposite the medical advice I received two and a half decades later upon delivering number twelve.

Aside from those remarkably brief discharge orders and the scant experience I'd scraped together babysitting in high school, everything I needed to know about caring for an infant was learned the hard way: through on-the-job training.

Yet the fleeting moments of self-doubt I experienced in my earliest days of mothering paled in comparison to the flood of apprehension and overwhelm that awaited me twenty-two months later when that same precious baby, emaciated and dehydrated, was diagnosed with type 1 diabetes shortly before his second birthday.

It took seven days at Children's Medical Center to stabilize him. And the exhaustive instructions and rigorous imperatives we received upon his discharge that time (not to mention the daunting supply of insulin, syringes, test strips, lancets, and glucose tabs) made those earlier tips on sponge baths and diaper creams look like child's play.

If his blood sugar dropped too low, he could die—same if it climbed too high. Thrice daily, we had to administer mixed doses of long- and short-acting insulin after predicting precisely how many carbohydrates our toddler would eat hours before he'd ingest them. Once mealtime arrived, if he turned up his nose at whatever was proffered, we had to race the clock to find something he'd swallow before his blood sugar tanked and he slipped into a coma.

The responsibility for keeping a tiny human alive seemed weighty during his first weeks of infancy. It felt crushingly heavy now.

Yet God is faithful! He preserved us. We survived, and so did our little boy. (He's grown and married now, with ten children of his own.)

Some folks claim God never gives you more than you can handle, but I've found the opposite to be true. God *routinely* gives us more than we can handle. It's His modus operandi—the way He naturally operates.

God loves using our weakness to showcase His strength—and doing it in a way that leaves no doubt whose strength we're leaning on amid what might otherwise be insurmountable odds.

In 2 Corinthians 12:9, God declares, "My grace is sufficient for you, for my power is made perfect in weakness."

I've tested this promise time and again—as have countless others facing far greater hardships—and can affirm: *God's mercy never fails!* (see Lamentations 3:21-23). And according to Matthew 7:7-11, He stands ready to lavish that same saving, sustaining grace on anyone and everyone who asks for it.

The Narrative

A WORLDLY RESPONSE TO "WORTH IT"	A BIBLICAL RESPONSE TO "WORTH IT"
Worries constantly if she is "enough"	Trusts in the "enoughness" of Christ's power at work within her
Gets so caught up in comparison that she gives up	Stays focused on the work God has called her to specifically
Shies away from practical efforts to improve	Looks for opportunities to connect with her children in new ways

Action Steps

- Memorize and meditate on Matthew 6:34: "Therefore do not be anxious about tomorrow, for tomorrow will be anxious for itself. Sufficient for the day is its own trouble."
- Make a list of two areas in which you connect well with your children and two areas that could use some improvement. Make a plan to do one practical thing to address one of those two problem areas this week.
- Write a list of moments of connection (grocery run, baking, reading a book, etc.) that you can say yes to (even though it would be easier to say no) and choose at least one to do this week.

Questions

Where does my anxiety that I'm not "doing enough" come from, and is there something I can do on a practical level to mute voices that produce fear rather than action?

What does the Bible have to say about investing well in our children?

How can I prioritize connection with my children this week?

Prayer

Father, thank You for the ways You pursue us with Your love. May Your patience and steadfastness, even in the face of our rebellion, be the example we strive to follow in discipling our children. And may we learn to rest in Your "enoughness." Amen.

CHAPTER 10

Mothering with a Legacy Mindset

One afternoon, as I scrolled through social media posts about a Christian women's conference, I somehow ended up on an unfamiliar account a friend who attended the event had tagged. As I glanced briefly through the woman's posts, one phrase caught my attention.

It was from a back-to-school post exhorting moms to use their newly freed-up time wisely in a worthwhile way that honored God. Great! I liked where this was heading.

But then the woman posting said this: "As you spend your time in ways that have greater impact than when your children are at home…" and my brain lurched to a halt. I circled back and read it again, certain I had misunderstood.

I can't guarantee I correctly interpreted her intent, but I wasn't wrong about the actual words, and what they seemed to imply was that having children at home is all well and good, but "kingdom work" begins when our time is free to do things of genuine worth. It's not even close to the first time I've encountered this mindset. I have an entire chapter on "The Profession of Motherhood" in

M Is for Mama that tackles the lie of the "someday" when our kids are in school, and we can actually "get real stuff done" and "exercise our true talents."

But what I'd like to address here is an increasingly shortsighted view of parenting that neglects to acknowledge the lasting effect our attitudes and actions have on our children (and their children and their children's children...you get the point). When we see and treat our kids as an investment of primary importance, we are imparting a legacy that is rooted in God's Word and richly reflective of His heart toward child training. Conversely, when we convey that discipling our children is a side project to our main gig or a distraction from more important work, we are passing down a legacy of an entirely different (and vastly inferior) sort.

Strength and Dignity

Once, as I filmed a segment for a series called "Parenting and Pornography: Roadmaps to Raising Children of Integrity" with Into the Light Ministries,[1] the young hosts kept using the phrase "vocational motherhood" as they talked about the responsibility parents have to teach our children about God's good design for sex. I found myself intrigued by the simple yet profound image those two words conjured.

I pictured a young woman dressed in cute-but-comfy clothes, hair atop her head in a messy bun, apron tied at her waist, with a dusting of flour on her nose, a whisk in one hand, a toddler gripped to her hip with the other, and a jaunty smile on her face. And then she morphed into a mom in her early forties, running her teenagers to sports practices, staying up late to listen when they suddenly become chatty before bed, secretly grinning that she's still the one they come to when they need wisdom. Of course, I could reshape that scene in my mind an infinitesimal number of times because a vocational mother can look like so many other things as well.

But in every version, the industriousness, the confidence, and the smile remain. Proverbs 31:25 (NLT) puts it this way: "She is clothed with strength and dignity, and she laughs without fear of the future."

In a culture that encourages women to be anything they'd like but balks at

VOCATIONAL
MOTHERHOOD
LEAVING A Legacy
INTENTIONALITY

the "anything" if it means prioritizing motherhood (a bit of a "you could be *anything*, and you chose *that*?" approach), the idea of viewing parenting as a vocation shines as a beacon of clarity for every mom and dad, regardless of any other pursuits they follow. For thousands of years, fathers and mothers have passed down the skills of their trades to their children, in hopes their offspring would, in turn, carry on the family business (or at the very least apply those skills profitably and diligently in a related area).

What if, instead of viewing our primary mothering season as a chore we check off for each child in eighteen years, we were to consider the incredible impact vocational parenting could have on the families of our children in their future? That, in faithfully discipling, teaching life skills, being affectionate, and simply having fun with our kids, we are setting them up with the parenting expertise they'll need, in turn, to invest well in their own children.

We're never guaranteed a particular outcome for our efforts (I'll talk more about this soon), but this is true of any endeavor with which we engage, so why not think beyond "making it to the end" and expand our vision to encompass a goal that includes generations to come?

Vocational Motherhood

In the spring of 2024, Kansas City Chiefs kicker, Harrison Butker, gave a commencement speech to a relatively small audience at a private Catholic college, but within hours, his words had spread throughout the world—namely due to what many labeled his polarizing (that was one of the nicest words used) views of women.

I read the entire speech and found much of it laudable, including the following snippet, which was scathingly criticized by mainstream news sources like CNN and Washington Post. They, along with a deluge of social media rants, all claimed that in describing the impact of his wife's choices on his own life, Butker was denigrating the worth of women everywhere.

This is what he said: "I can tell you that my beautiful wife, Isabelle, would be the first to say that her life truly started when she began living her vocation as a wife and as a mother. I'm on this stage today and able to be the man I am because I have a wife who leans into her vocation."[2]

(There's that word again.)

Most took especial umbrage at the phrase "her life truly started," and while I'll be the first to confirm that our lives have great value before we become wives and mothers (assuming marriage and motherhood are even on our horizon), I wonder if the response would have been just as rabidly negative if a female astrophysicist had said, "My life truly started when I landed a job at NASA."

My gut feeling? Probably not.

Why?

Because when we hear a statement like this from a woman who is seen as having reached the pinnacle of her career's achievements and has the degree and the paycheck to show for it, we have been conditioned to stand up and slow clap. *That* is a woman who has taken her legacy seriously. She's contributing to the world in meaningful ways. If only we could have more of her kind.

We understand her declaration of "my life truly started" to be one of passion and appreciation for her role, not of exclusion to any other purpose in her life.

So why such a different response when the passion and the purpose prioritize motherhood? Why is that choice "oppression" and "servitude" (yep, those words were used multiple times) and the other empowerment? And why was the same outrage not applied to the portion of Butker's speech that referenced one of his Super Bowl wins and then continued with "none of these accomplishments mean anything compared to the happiness I have found in my marriage and in starting a family. My confidence...is rooted in marriage with my wife, as we leave our mark on future generations by the children we bring into the world"? After all, shouldn't those offended by his reference to his wife's prioritizing parenting also object to his downplaying his own professional accomplishments in favor of familial duties? And yet, they did not.

And the reason, my friends, lies at the bottom of a rabbit hole of feminism down which we do not have time to tunnel at the moment.

But I will say this: If more men and women were encouraged to view parenthood as a vocation with an everlasting impact rather than something to tack onto the "stuff that actually matters," we would truly have a reason to stand up and cheer.

If more men and women were encouraged to view parenthood as a vocation with an everlasting impact rather than something to tack onto the "stuff that actually matters," we would truly have a reason to stand up and cheer.

And I say this as someone who, on a very personal level, has had to work through the tension between loving being a mom and also loving being lots of other things too. I almost can't believe I didn't include in either of my previous books the story of how I came to be known as "M Is for Mama," but now seems like a good time to reveal how the phrase came to be my blog's title, my social media handle, my podcast name—my brand, so to speak.

"M" Is for Mama

Over a decade ago, when my twin girls were babies, I wandered into a cute boutique in my hometown, searching for a small gold disc with an *S* on it as a gift for my mom. She goes by the name Softa (a play on the Hebrew word for "grandma"), and I wanted to find a charm for a necklace I'd bought her.

Sadly, they were all out of her namesake letter, but just as I turned to leave, I noticed a disc with the letter *M* swaying gently on its display and, without a fully formed thought, picked it up and bought it.

Afterward, I sat in my car, rubbing the small metal circle between my thumb and forefinger, trying to pinpoint the impulse that had prompted me to spend money on it. As I did, these were the thoughts that formed, clearly and cogently, in my mind: "You get more excited about telling people you used to be a high school Spanish teacher than you do telling them you're now a homeschooling mom of five—not because you actually prefer the first vocation to the second but because 'they' express more respect and admiration for you when they hear you're a foreign language teacher than they do when they hear you're 'just' a mom. This is so backward. You genuinely believe your impact to be greater at home than it was in the classroom. You even blog about it. So why don't you just embrace it wholeheartedly?"

I put the *M* around my neck on a simple gold chain and wore it for years (I still do sometimes). And every time someone's eye would catch on the letter, and they would ask, "Why do you wear an *M*? I thought your name was Abbie," I'd say, "*M* is for Mama. It's a reminder of my primary purpose right now and what a privilege it is to hold that title."

It never failed to produce a reaction—usually a positive one. If the person asking was a mom, she'd usually pause with a slightly startled expression before a slow smile spread across her face, and she'd begin to nod her head vigorously in agreement. (I even had a few friends who adopted the practice as well.) Sometimes we just need a tangible reminder of the precious gift it is to steward souls.

As a result of this mindset shift, more people around the world know me as "Mama" than Abbie, not because I have always been impervious to the allure of being "something more important than just a mom" but because I know it all too well. And the Lord nudged me through that very temptation to shy away from declaring the importance of my role toward confidence in the vocation He has set before me as a pursuit to bring glory to Him and bless my family.

Along the way, He has granted me incredible opportunities to encourage other moms to do the same. I get to do this in my own home from a living room chair or a "girl cave" couch, or stuffed into the cracks of naptimes and quiet times, or times when Shaun says, "Go write, I've got this" or I hire my girls to help out with their toddler brothers. To the young moms chafing at the bit to "do something that matters," I say, "You already are."

Yes, I'm grateful for the opportunity to share with you now, many years after the desire to do so first blossomed in my heart. But I'm under no delusion this impact trumps the one I have at home. It doesn't. And I will never tire of declaring motherhood worth boldly claiming as a legacy vocation.

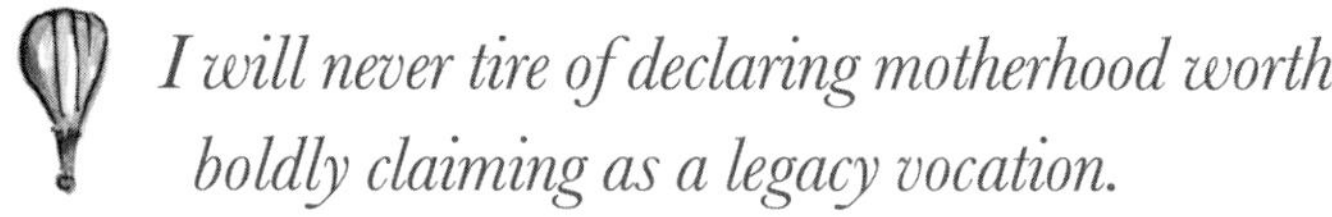

I will never tire of declaring motherhood worth boldly claiming as a legacy vocation.

My Mama, the Trailblazer

Speaking of legacy, I am privileged to have a mother who has modeled this mindset for me well.

My mama has a master's degree in English and taught for years at both the high school and collegiate levels. She has an intimidating IQ and a formidable will to shape culture. She was on the front lines of the movement to legalize homeschooling in Texas (imagine fighting for your right to educate the children you carried, birthed, fed, and clothed), was politically active in her community, proving instrumental in effecting policies that banned the public display of pornographic materials in convenience stores in our town, and even started her own small homeschool co-op when I was a teen so she could continue to invest in my education while bringing in a modest side income for our family.

She is, to be a bit cliché about it, a force to be reckoned with.

Once I started college at fifteen (heavily guided and aided by my mom's knowledge of the enrollment process and pursuit of academic and financial scholarships), she moved from part-time to full-time work. And yet I never doubted her commitment to her family first. Many would consider her focus on my brother and me during our formative years a waste of her degrees. But my mom viewed her education as a vehicle to help provide for her family and to funnel her knowledge into the two people she considered most worthy of her attention, *while* remaining community-minded.

And that commitment remains, as she continues to prioritize her family by making herself available to both my brother and me in whatever capacity we need. She has done this since our combined fourteen children first began arriving almost twenty years ago. But in the last ten years, for my family, this has looked like hiring her to come two days a week for six hours a day to do whatever needs doing.

Some have asked me why we need to pay her, since she is my mom, but the truth is, we feel a responsibility to honor her desire to invest in her grandchildren and adult children by keeping her from needing to work for someone else instead.

Of course, no amount of money could truly repay her for the efforts and time she pours into us, which go far beyond the twelve hours a week she spends at my house. My mom has helped my children learn to do fractions, scrubbed my toilets, rocked my babies to sleep, held the fort when Shaun and I travel, washed my dishes, planted my flower beds, made dinner, taken her grandchildren with her to do errands, and too many other "little" things that would wreck my allotted word count for this book.

So why does she do all these things? Because she believes her legacy did not end when my brother and I moved out. And, as someone who lost two grandparents at an early age and had two others who weren't very interested in relationships with their grandchildren, I can attest to the difference it has made in my children's lives.

They adore Softa and literally cheer each time she pulls up in our driveway, eager to hug her, raid her purse for gum, and hang on her arm, catching her up on the bugs they've caught, treats they've baked, chapters they've written, and workouts they've crushed since the last time she saw them (usually within the past forty-eight hours).

I'm fully cognizant of the rare, invaluable gem this ongoing relationship with my mom is to our family (my brother feels the same way), but my dad and Shaun's parents are also invested in our families (although our contact is not as consistent). Having four grandparents who support and cheer us on in our efforts to raise up a family in the "discipline and instruction of the Lord" (Ephesians 6:4) is almost unheard of in a culture that encourages empty nesters to "finally get back to living your best life for yourself."

Telling the Next Generation

I hear from so many young moms whose own mothers express dismay when they announce their pregnancies, telling them, "I hope you're not expecting me to babysit. I have a life, you know." I've received dozens of messages from moms telling me my books have served as a de facto mentor in their lives, and while I'm so grateful to encourage and exhort sisters in Christ, it saddens me they are unable to find anyone (including their own mothers) willing to disciple them in a face-to-face capacity.

I truly believe this is due to an all-ages-included epidemic of myopic self-focus that fails to grasp the urgency conveyed in Psalm 78:2-4 (NIV), which says, "I will utter hidden things, things from of old—things we have heard and known, things our ancestors have told us. We will not hide them from their descendants; we will tell the next generation the praiseworthy deeds of the LORD, his power, and the wonders he has done."

Imagine if all Christian parents took this passage to heart in word and deed!

Here's the thing: We can fixate on the failures of our ancestors, or we can accept our responsibility to turn the tide, regardless of how ill-equipped we feel to build a legacy from the ground up by the grace of God.

I talk in more detail about my own parents' dedication to forsaking their less-than-stellar backgrounds in order to forge ahead into the uncharted territory of biblical vocational parenting in chapters 7 and 8 of *Hard Is Not the Same Thing as Bad*. And while my parents made plenty of mistakes along the way (as every parent will), they still laid a foundation on which my brother and I can build, and for that I am forever grateful.

If they can do it, so can you. If you are reading this chapter filled with envy for the leg up on legacy motherhood my mama gave me, keep in mind you are only one layer removed from her choice. Yes, it's harder to be the trailblazer than the trail maintainer, but change has to start somewhere, so if not with your ancestors, may it be with you!

Because I know many of you are wondering what this could look like on a practical level (and some of you feel like you've been handed an intentional legacy that you don't want to mess up, but you feel a bit lost about how to stay strong in the fight), I've included some suggestions for ways to consistently and purposefully invest in a family culture that will, Lord willing, be the gift that keeps on giving for generations to come.

Family Bible Reading

It sounds so basic, but keep in mind that foundations (think concrete, bricks, and cinder blocks) are rarely flashy or intricate. Instead, they are simple and solid. The goal here is this: "Everyone then who hears these words of mine and does them will be like a wise man who built his house on the rock. And the rain fell, and the floods came, and the winds blew and beat on that house, but it did not fall, because it had been founded on the rock" (Matthew 7:24-25).

When we build any legacy on the solid rock of Christ and His Holy Word, we know our foundation is sure and unshakable. But we do ourselves a disservice when we make laying this foundation so complicated that we'll never actually follow through on it.

When we build any legacy on the solid rock of Christ and His Holy Word, we know our foundation is sure and unshakable.

Our Bible reading consists of our entire family gathering together in our living room at 7:30 a.m. to read a chapter from the Old Testament and a chapter from the New Testament and then pray together (each member of our family prays in order of birth, from youngest to oldest). Shaun stops frequently to ask questions of varying age levels for clarification and comprehension. He has the kids restate key verses in their own words (a practice called narration, which helps to solidify concepts in our minds) to make sure they've grasped the essentials. He chooses verses from our readings to memorize together as a family (a process that can be as simple as his saying a phrase and then all of us repeating it after him until we begin to grasp it and then practicing again the next day). And he jots down questions from the reading for our Sunday night Bible Buzzers trivia game.

Whenever I share our family Bible-reading routine, I get a deluge of questions:

"Do you do this every morning?"

No, but we strive to be consistent.

"What translation do you use?"

We use the ESV, but if you're new to Bible reading, the NLT is a great paraphrase for readability without losing important biblical accuracy.

"Has Shaun always led this?"

No, I actually did a version of this for years before he felt convicted and confident to take over. If your husband's not there yet, I encourage you to faithfully lead your children in this area as you pray for the Lord to embolden and equip your husband.

"What do you do about the confusing parts or the parts that reference sex and violence?"

We read them as they're written, and then we discuss them in an age-appropriate way; remember, it's absolutely fine to tell your children, "I don't know the answer to that question, but I can try to find out" and then read a book or a commentary or talk with a trusted pastor or advisor for further wisdom before you get back to them.

"Does everybody sit quietly?"

No, there's a fair bit of wiggling and whispering from restless littles, but we persevere, firm in the knowledge that faithful practice will produce progress (not perfection) in family devotions just as it does in everything else.

"Do I have to do it at the same time you do, in the same room of the house you do, with the same version you do, and the same number of kids you do, in the same tone of voice you do for it to work?"

Okay, now I'm just being silly, but it is almost comical how detailed my readers' questions can get (especially those who've never established this habit for themselves and are terrified of "doing it wrong").

Friends, take a deep breath, shake your shoulders out, and repeat after me: "The Lord is pleased with my efforts to honor Him by reading His Word with my family, and He will give me wisdom about how to do it best."

If that means evening instead of morning, using a children's Bible with very small children (I recommend *The Complete Illustrated Children's Bible*, both for content and for beautiful illustrations), learning Scripture through song, or any other biblically sound tweaks you need to make to tailor the experience for your family, I say go for it! May the Holy Spirit be your guide. Just start somewhere!

Family Traditions

One of the most practical ways we can build strong family cultures that our children will want to pass down to their children after them is to cultivate consistent traditions.

One of the most practical ways we can build strong family cultures that our children will want to pass down to their children after them is to cultivate consistent traditions.

My friend Susan is the queen of traditions in her home. Each holiday has its own special meal, even down to the meatloaf baked in a heart-shaped pan for Valentine's Day. She's created rituals for birthdays and milestones that feel like "home" to her clan, resulting in even adult children who rearrange their schedules around the holidays so they can be home for the festivities.

If that's not your jam, maybe you're more like my friend Jennifer (whom you heard from in the last chapter), who's made travel such an interwoven element of their family's fabric that her adult children still join them for trips whenever their schedule or work allows.

My husband still speaks of a family he knew during his teenage years whose traditions revolved around books, books, and more books. They read individual books together in the same room, read aloud collectively, and discussed what they were reading at the dinner table. Imagine how many inside jokes and shared memories they have over scenes from *Huckleberry Finn* or *The Secret Garden* or *The Hobbit.*

Our family has a smorgasbord of several of these elements (as, I'm sure, do the families I've mentioned). I love to read aloud to my children, and they love it too. We love to travel together. And we have tried-and-true traditions that surface at specific holidays, without which we would feel lost.

We also have quirky conventions like our semiannual "Family Bake-Off" (where the boys and the girls compete to bake a themed confection, and then we invite friends over to judge our efforts), epic Nertz competitions (only the best speed card game ever), and movie nights on our DIY "big screen" (we made it by sanding down a large wall until smooth, painting it flat white, and then framing it with black trim).

If you don't see anything that resonates with you from any of these examples, that's perfectly fine. I encourage you to pray about the traditions the Lord might inspire you to create to help anchor your children's hearts to home. All the better if you already have wonderful ones passed down from your forefathers and mothers, but don't be afraid to get the ball rolling if you don't.

Imagine the day your own grandchildren help you put together care packages for those in need each Thanksgiving or giddily pull out the cookie cutters reserved just for Christmas Eve baking. What a thrill to know you've contributed to the development of memory-building practices that help undergird a lasting family heritage.

Family Rhythms

Similar to the common concerns of not enjoying and not feeling listened to by your own children that I addressed in chapter 7, I often hear from moms who feel like their schedules are running them rather than the other way around.

They don't have strong, consistent rhythms in place for establishing peace and reasonable expectations in their home, and they wake up dreading the day or feeling lost about what they should be doing next to make a lasting impact on their children's hearts and, by extension, behavior.

One of the best things you can do for yourself and even generations to come is to prioritize a handful of simple, repetitive practices that set you up for success throughout your day—a win you can build on over the course of weeks, months, and years as you grow your capacity for consistency and responsibility.

One of the best things you can do for yourself and even generations to come is to prioritize a handful of simple, repetitive practices that set you up for success throughout your day.

If these practices don't come naturally to you, let me assure you I'm not talking about complicated schedules or routines.

In fact, I choose the word "rhythm" very intentionally because it has such a gentle connotation of flow rather than rigidity. Rhythms can easily be adjusted during pregnancy, postpartum periods, and just about any other life eventuality, without being lost altogether.

I'll share with you some of my own personal rhythms as an example (because I know y'all love it when I get specific), but just as with our family Bible reading, these practices are particular to my life's needs and are subject to change depending on the season in which I find myself.

Currently, during summer break:

Wake at 6:30

Start a load of laundry

Read and journal a passage from my One Year Chronological Bible

Make breakfast for myself, Shaun, and the smaller children (the older children prefer to make their own)

Teach a class at the gym (I take the twinbies and Shiloh with me)

Pick up a grocery order on the way home from the gym
Make lunch for myself and the smallest children
Flip the laundry from the washer to the dryer and start a new load
Put the twinbies down for a nap
Work (either on income-producing tasks or on housework)
Read aloud to the kids who are awake while they fold clothes
Make dinner
Flip the laundry one more time
Hang out with family
Take a shower with Shaun (we love this time together to talk through our day with zero interruptions)
Go to bed

I realize this is more of a play-by-play than a "few simple rhythms" throughout my day, but if you skim the highlights, you'll notice there's a flow of Bible time, food, exercise, work, and time with my family.

I intentionally didn't list specific times for each of these activities (other than waking up) because they can vary per day and demands on my time. But knowing that most days will include a combination of at least three of these elements helps me to wake up with purpose and direction.

I also know these personal rhythms inform the rhythms of my children (who have specific times and jobs for morning and evening cleanups, quiet times in the afternoon, and plenty of free play) and that my example of consistency (not perfection) will help them establish their own priorities for personal and family rhythms in the future.

If you feel lost on how to know what to prioritize, I encourage you to write down a typical day in your home, like I just did, and study it to notice the things that emerge as patterns or the things that feel like they *should* be there but are missing at the moment.

And then choose one area at a time on which to focus as you develop consistent cadences in your own family. If you desire to leave a legacy of a calm and joyful home environment to your children (which can look different for every family), it's possible, no matter what your natural personality bent.

And, as always, mute the clamorous voices of comparison and those that claim the *only* way to honor God on a Sunday morning is to have breakfast prepped to go in the oven first thing in the morning, a meal in the crockpot for lunch, all the outfits laid out the night before, and your hair and makeup done an hour before the kids get up. If this is you, great job! If it's not, but you still show up to worship God each week, and you've found a rhythm that allows you to do that with sanity intact, good for you! Way to persevere and make decisions that benefit your family!

Friends, I want to encourage you that leaving a legacy for generations to come need not be a daunting prospect. Why? Because we don't determine the outcome. We faithfully plant the seeds and trust the Lord to bring the harvest.

I want to encourage you that leaving a legacy for generations to come need not be a daunting prospect. Why? Because we don't determine the outcome. We faithfully plant the seeds and trust the Lord to bring the harvest.

What a freeing and exciting opportunity to shape generations to come simply by our commitment to buck the culture's emphasis on *self* and *instant gratification* over faithful investment. Your line in the sand now can become the Ebenezer that your great-grandchildren point to one day and say, "This is where it all began."

So why not start today?

A Titus Two Perspective

BETH ANDERSON
mother of two (including Abbie),
best Softa in the world

Psalm 145:4 declares, "One generation shall praise Your works to another, and shall declare Your mighty acts" (NKJV).

Even though I come from a long line of gardeners, I'm still in awe of how things grow. When I put a tomato seed into the soil, that seed rots, dies, and disappears. But then a plant comes up, which eventually produces more tomatoes than I can make into salsa, each tomato full of seeds, and each seed containing the potential for infinite fruit.

During the Great Depression, after each year's vegetable harvest, my grandfather would handpick his seeds for the next year's planting. Feeding his family depended on preserving these seeds, and he made sure the best seeds were saved for next year's garden. The Lord's role for parents resembles my grandfather's conscientiousness with his Depression-era garden. God desires families who live out His values to continue for generations, and He wants their members to abide with Him forever.

To propagate a harvest of righteousness, God has designed the family with a dynamic of dependency. Parents are instructed by the Lord to rear *His* children—*whom He entrusts to us*—with an eternal perspective. We watch, guard, guide, filter, discipline, sacrifice, persevere, and pray, ardently looking to Him for guidance.

We pray for, support, and enjoy our kids' endeavors. And we are happy when they honor us, including listening to our counsel. But eventually, they must answer directly to the Holy Spirit. Teaching them diligently can be repetitive—and demanding (see Deuteronomy 6:7). And so we pray that God's truths fall on receptive hearts and minds.

Raising children demands sacrifice, but the Lord alone produces life. Our kids will have to learn some good, true things the hard way; all seeds must die to bear fruit (John 12:24). Shepherding children can be exhausting, frustrating, and scary, but we are not to live in fear and worry. Jesus Himself is our peace (Ephesians 2:14). When we stay focused on Him as our hope and strength, He will honor our faith—in His time (Hebrews 6:16-19, 1 Peter 1:3-7, and Ecclesiastes 3:11).

I must deliberately plant and carefully cultivate vegetables and flowers in my garden, whereas weeds multiply exponentially with almost no water and certainly no tending. In our desire to pass on a legacy of blessing, we need to unapologetically parent with intentionality. We must challenge—or, as Paul says, wage war against—entrenched generational sin patterns through repentance (see 2 Corinthians 10:2-6). Although we aren't responsible for our parents' mistakes, we still have to deal with the consequences of their choices—including the weeds they let grow. To turn curses into blessings, we must emphasize Scripture, encourage wholesome influences, and *re*-reiterate the bread-and-butter biblical basics:

- **Fear only the Lord** (Proverbs 9:10 and Romans 14:23).
- **Persevere** (Psalm 27 and Isaiah 40:31).
- **Saturate your mind with God's Word** (Romans 12:2 and Isaiah 26:3).
- **Repent daily** (1 John 1:9).
- **Grow in grace and gratefulness** (2 Peter 3:18).
- **Pray always** (Ephesians 6:18).
- **Cherish Jesus's love and mercy** (1 Corinthians 13:8).

As with plant life, spiritual survival takes more than the best human efforts. The yield from our hard work does not compare with God-given supernatural life and growth. If raising good seeds depended only on us, we would be surrounded by dirt and weeds. But when we rely on God, we will see the potential for infinite fruit. For it is *His* heritage, *His* garden, *His* seed, for *His* glory alone (see Romans 11:36).

> "I am the true vine, and my Father is the gardener...If you remain in me and I in you, you will bear much fruit; apart from me you can do nothing" (John 15:1, 5 NIV).

The Narrative

A WORLDLY RESPONSE TO "WORTH IT"	A BIBLICAL RESPONSE TO "WORTH IT"
Considers motherhood an "add-on" to "more important stuff"	Recognizes motherhood as a vocation of primary importance
Fixates on the here-and-now struggles of the everyday	Thinks ahead to the potential impact on future generations
Feels overwhelmed by the prospect of generational legacy	Welcomes the opportunity to lay a foundation of righteousness for her children's children

Action Steps

- Memorize and meditate on Psalm 78:2-4 (NIV): "I will utter hidden things, things from of old—things we have heard and known, things our ancestors have told us. We will not hide them from their descendants; we will tell the next generation the praiseworthy deeds of the LORD, his power, and the wonders he has done."
- Write your own definition of the phrase "legacy motherhood."
- Make a list of three things (positive or negative) passed down to you from your own mother or guardian.

Questions

In what ways are you embracing a mindset of "vocational motherhood"? In what ways are you not?

How do you feel about the three things you listed previously that were passed down to you from your ancestors? Do you want to pass them down to your own children?

Why is it important to think beyond today (or this week or month or year, even) when it comes to choosing to view motherhood as a worthy vocation?

Prayer

Lord, even if we were not given a godly legacy, we still have the opportunity in Your strength to change that for our own children. Give us clear eyes for the future to understand the lasting impact that leaning into vocational motherhood can have on our own children and generations to come. Amen.

CHAPTER 11

What to Do When You've Grown Weary of Doing Good

When my friend and volunteer editor, Jennifer, heard I was writing my second book, *Hard Is Not the Same Thing as Bad*, she wasn't surprised. She knows me well and already knew this phrase as the heartbeat of what I preach to myself and fellow mamas daily.

But she did have this word of caution: "Abbie, you can't write a book with this title and not expect to experience some hardship in the process."

I acknowledged the truth of her statement, not from a place of trepidation but from experience.

Just as we're usually granted opportunities to practice rather than being given a spiritual IV of patience or gentleness or self-control when we ask the Lord to grow us in these areas, we almost never get to declare biblical truths to others without first taking them for a test-drive ourselves (and then continuing with them in a daily commute of sanctification).

To be clear, I had absolutely already experienced challenges and struggles before I wrote a book about the ways the Lord uses the hard things in our life to transform us from "wish I could" to "doing it because it's right, even when I'm scared or don't like it."

Still, I could not have predicted the path the Lord would lay before our family beginning twelve days before *Hard Is Not the Same Thing as Bad* launched into the world.

At 6:40 a.m., on August 23, 2023, I walked down our stairs, groggily wondering why my oldest son had left the water running as he got ready for work that morning, and stepped into a shallow lake in our living room. Everywhere I looked, the surface of our floors glistened with an inch of water.

Turns out, a hose had burst underneath our sink the night before, and 90 percent of our downstairs was flooded.

Our family worked together for several hours to mop, sweep, and squeegee the water out of the first floor, and only then did we receive the disheartening news from a mold remediation crew that we would lose all the affected flooring, baseboards (and adjoining trim), all lower kitchen cabinets, and all attached poured-in-place DIY concrete countertops. Honestly, my brain wasn't capable of processing much more than sending short commands to my muscles to wring out a towel or vacuum up a bit more water by that point.

When I did have a moment to reflect, though, this is what I thought: "Okay, Lord. I know You're sovereign. I know You'll use this for our good and Your glory. But did it have to happen *now*?"

Before the flood, I had already been girding my loins for a daunting fall semester that included homeschooling, a book launch, a launch party attended by hundreds, several travel obligations, and the always busy holiday season.

I certainly didn't have "deal with a house flood/move into a rental/renovate the entire downstairs" on my preferred-circumstances bingo card for the fall.

And yet? As I contemplated the reality that there's never really a "good time" to have a house flood (or any other struggle, for that matter), I felt an assurance of the Lord's care settle on my shoulders like a comforting blanket.

That abiding sense of assurance returned over and over throughout a year that included everything I've already mentioned but also four months of debilitating, unexplained back pain (stress, much?), multiple renovation delays, which resulted in six months of living in a rental (a blessing to have, but also not without its challenges), a spring that revealed deep heartache in the form of multiple crises with extended family, and a summer that began with joy at the news of expecting a new baby and ended with the crushing and confusing reality of a missed miscarriage.

In truth, I write these words to you immediately after a second sonogram appointment we made for the express purpose of confirming what we were already fairly certain of: that though I should have been ten weeks pregnant, our baby had stopped growing at six weeks, and my body had not gotten the message yet to start the physical miscarriage process.

I do not write from a place of solely fulfilled expectations or answered prayers tied up in a pretty bow.

I write from a position of what has felt like a long season of being dunked in the sometimes turbulent waters of God's sovereignty time and again, only to emerge gasping and clinging to my tiny craft of Faith, knowing I need not a magnificent vessel to stay afloat—but rather to trust in the One who steers the boat, regardless of its size or majesty.

Did we also experience sweet times amidst the struggles? So, so many, friends.

What an incredible year it was of unexpected opportunities to share God's goodness with a wider audience, travel and make memories as a family, and grow in our confidence in the Lord's kind attention to the tiniest details of our lives!

And yet, just as Jennifer warned me, hardship was, indeed, a theme.

What First?

I share all this because I know many of you are walking through challenges that weren't on your preferred-circumstances bingo card either.

You wouldn't have chosen for your husband to lose his job right before Christmas, for the cancer diagnosis to have come back positive, for your adult child to have made the life choices he did, for the much-hoped-for dream to have shriveled into a mere shadow of its former glory until it dies quietly in a corner.

I get it.

When it comes to mothering well in Christ's strength, one of the most sobering realities is we *will need* His help. The truth is, we always do. But we recognize this most when our last-ditch efforts to curb our preteen's rude speech have fallen flat. When we feel like we might go stark raving mad if the baby refuses to sleep again tonight. When we find ourselves doubting everything we thought we knew about parenting because our eight-year-old won't stop lying.

Romans 12:12 reminds us to "rejoice in hope, be patient in tribulation, be constant in prayer," which is a far cry from the knee-jerk reaction so many (me too sometimes!) have to hardships: giving in to despair, wishing trouble away immediately, and complaining far more often than we pray.

One of my favorite anchor verses as a parent is Galatians 6:9, which exhorts us to "not grow weary of doing good, for in due season we will reap, if we do not give up." I've lost track of how many times I've grabbed hold of this verse to undergird a spiritual principle of perseverance in the midst of a hard parenting morning, month, or year.

But I can't deny readers have shot back many times in return, "But what if I *have* grown weary of doing good? What then?"

Our efforts often don't feel worth it when we don't see immediate results. Our patience can wear paper-thin when we've been promised a particular outcome and received something much less fulfilling instead (I'll talk more soon about the kinds of parenting philosophies that can lead to this kind of burnout). We can feel hopeless when there's no obvious end to the struggle.

So, what then?

I would like to posit that "What then?" is not the best question to ask at such a moment. It implies that, after exhausting all of our options, we stand at the precipice of a cliff, with no choice but to jump to certain doom, the next and inevitable step.

Instead, what if we were to ask ourselves, "What first?"

If that sounds a bit confusing, let me explain.

Following a destructive path to its logical conclusion is not our only choice in the Christian life. Even if we've fallen into repetitive negative habits or thought patterns, even if we've run out of parenting steam, even if nothing we do seems to make any impression on our children's character or choices, this fact remains: Because we have Christ, we have hope.

And hope says we can begin anew to pursue the needful things each and every day. We do not have to take the next step off the cliff of our failures or disappointments. We can forge a new path by making the simple (yet difficult) choice to believe "the Lord is pleased with those who fear Him, who hope in His loving devotion" (Psalm 147:11 BSB). Because when we prioritize our relationship with the Lord *first*, every bit of our parenting is informed by that choice.

The following principles are not a foolproof prescription to restore your parenting vigor if you've grown weary of doing good, but each truth I share here appears multiple times throughout the pages of God's Word, and His Word never returns void. So I feel confident of pointing you toward not a wide, smooth path of ease (a good thing, too, since Matthew 7:13 assures us that path leads to destruction), but a narrow one of purpose and the kind of joy that makes no sense unless it comes from Jesus.

Anticipate Struggle (but Also Great Reward)

Just like the mom I mentioned way back in chapter 1 who, having grown up with affluence and ease, felt disillusioned by the constant demands of motherhood and concluded she should've skipped having children altogether, we can easily fall prey to the fantasy that our lives could be completely stress free if only we didn't have these small (or big) humans needing us all the time.

The truth?

We know from Jesus's words in John 16:33 that we *will* have trouble in this world, regardless of whether we are single, married, widowed, childless, or blessed with fifteen kids.

If, instead of approaching motherhood with the expectation of smooth sailing all the time, we anticipate the kinds of storms that grow our faith, increase our capacity for struggle, and teach us new skills, then we're neither surprised nor shaken when such storms inevitably arise.

If, instead of approaching motherhood with the expectation of smooth sailing all the time, we anticipate the kinds of storms that grow our faith, increase our capacity for struggle, and teach us new skills, then we're neither surprised nor shaken when such storms inevitably arise.

Not only that, but we receive great reward for our perseverance. And we know this because the Bible tells us, "Blessed is the man who perseveres under trial, because when he has stood the test, he will receive the crown of life that God has promised to those who love Him" (James 1:12 BSB).

This holds true in light of eternity with Christ, which is the ultimate reward, but also in short-term joys like sinking our teeth into that first luscious bite of fresh, butter-soaked bread we baked with our children after pushing through meltdowns over who gets to stir the dough, flour dumped on the floor, and at least one broken dish.

Earlier in that same chapter, James 1:2-4 encourages us to "count it all joy… when you meet trials of various kinds, for you know that the testing of your faith produces steadfastness. And let steadfastness have its full effect, that you may be perfect and complete, lacking in nothing."

If perfection and completion sound like the opposite of what you're currently experiencing in parenting, the problem may not be your children or even your circumstances, but instead unrealistic expectations of ease coupled with a lack of steadfastness in the face of the hardship the Bible tells us *every* Christian will face.

Mindset Matters

What if, instead of thinking, "I can't believe my toddler needs to go potty right after bedtime again," we thought, "I'm grateful he didn't have an accident in his undies. He's making progress!"

What if, instead of bemoaning the fact that our preteen never stops talking, we reminded ourselves of what a privilege it is to be the one in whom she confides?

What if, instead of rolling our eyes every time our seven-year-old says, "Mom, watch," we took a moment to stop and encourage him, knowing, one day, he'll be much more interested in impressing a girl that's not his mom?

What if, instead of feeling resentful at the thought of making dinner again, we praised God for the opportunity to fill bellies and nourish souls?

All these scenarios (and so many more I could list) are examples of mindset shifts. They're a practice you might find in any number of self-help books, but the root of the principle for believers comes from Romans 12:2, which says, "Do not be conformed to this world, but be transformed by the renewal of your mind, that by testing you may discern what is the will of God, what is good and acceptable and perfect."

"This world" assures us complaining is the ticket to emotional release. A huge parenting account, whose creator regularly exhorts her followers to "get yourself a snack" (which is not bad advice), also regularly makes posts about how the harder aspects of motherhood "suck." She fashions herself a parenting tour guide who drives the bus of "reality, not that shiny, fake $#!* you're being sold on some accounts" and assures her readers that everyone is welcome to ride along with zero judgment for their angst toward their families.

It's so tempting to climb aboard the Bellyaching Bus.

But then, 1 Thessalonians 5:18 hits us square between the eyes with this: "Give thanks in all circumstances; for this is the will of God in Christ Jesus for you."

In other words, when social media tells us we're entitled to stay stuck in the woe-is-me spiral of victimhood, God's Word encourages us we have a choice to "take every thought captive to obey Christ" (2 Corinthians 10:5).

That kind of Spirit-filled agency is the perfect antidote to the endless loop of "I can't; I'm too tired" that threatens to torpedo our best intentions. (And I write this from a place of mental, emotional, and physical depletion, so I know whereof I speak.)

After all, "I can because Jesus will supply all I need" is the best mindset shift for every area of life.

Fear God, Not Circumstances

One of the consistent themes of the messages I get from overwhelmed moms is a focus on the current (or potential) struggle rather than a future hope of glory with Christ. We've already said we're to expect the hardship. But what if, once it's here, it's all you can see, and you find yourself terrified of the outcome more than fearing (in the biblical sense) the Outcome Determiner?

If you're wondering what good "future glory" does for your "right now," let me assure you, in this moment, the hope of a heavenly reunion with my sweet baby (who joins three others we never got to hold on earth) is the primary comfort for my heart as I grieve the opportunity to caress downy hair and kiss silky cheeks. The earthly outcome was not the one I hoped and prayed for. But the One who gave me that little baby to briefly carry, safe and loved, is the same One who now carries my precious child, free from care, sorrow, sin, and pain.

Looking forward to the "eternal weight of glory beyond all comparison" promised to believers in 2 Corinthians 4:16-18 informs our patience as we parent, knowing each day invested in our families "for the Lord" (Colossians 3:23) brings us closer to hearing "Well done, good and faithful servant" (Matthew 25:23), closer to leaving earthly sorrows behind, closer to an eternity with the Lord.

The wrinkle? Fearing God and working heartily for Him more than for any human (including our children or ourselves) requires us to peel our eyes off our less-than-stellar circumstances and acknowledge that, though we may never get the results we think we deserve here on earth, Colossians 3:24 promises that "from the Lord you will receive the inheritance as your reward. You are serving the Lord Christ."

There's that eternal reward again! Of course, one of the quickest and surest ways of growing weary in doing good is to allow the world to cow us into a culturally acceptable view of success that focuses on wealth, academic achievements, and beauty.

One of the quickest and surest ways of growing weary in doing good is to allow the world to cow us into a culturally acceptable view of success that focuses on wealth, academic achievements, and beauty.

We tell ourselves if we're not seeing these benchmarks, we must be failing, or God must be failing us. The fear of falling short of man's standards leads to confusion and resentment when we inevitably do exactly that in some way or with that one child.

By contrast, Proverbs 9:10 assures us "the fear of the LORD is the beginning of wisdom"—an encouraging prospect since so much of burnout comes from feeling like we don't have the discernment or knowledge we need to move forward.

Do the Next Thing

Very little cripples our resolve to rejoice and be thankful faster than feeling stuck. Stuck in our current cycle of self-defeating habits, stuck in a whirlpool of self-doubt and recrimination, stuck in a house we don't like, stuck in a difficult marriage.

If the fear of the Lord is the *beginning* of wisdom, what is its completion?

The answer might be simpler (though, not necessarily easier) than you think.

I originally titled this section "Do the Next Right Thing." I'm aware this concept is not unique to me, but it is something I remind myself of often that helps me get *unstuck* from a fixation on frustrating circumstances.

DO THE NEXT THING

But then I remembered how Elisabeth Elliot spoke often and candidly of the unexpected roles and stresses thrust upon her after her husband, Jim, was murdered by the Auca tribe in Ecuador. She also referenced the paralysis that can come when we try to zoom out from our current circumstances, frantically scanning the horizon for closure, rather than asking God to shine His light on the next few feet of the path He has asked us to walk.

Her solution?

Do the next thing.

And I decided *this* was the phrase to head up this section. Because adding the word "right" throws a moral shading onto what is so often a practical necessity. Inevitably, if I say, "Do the next right thing," someone will respond, "But how do I know that it's right?"

By contrast, the plain encouragement to "do the next thing" takes the guesswork out of the situation.

When you wake up, your children need to eat, and so you do the next thing of making breakfast.

When your clothes are dirty, you do the next thing of starting a load of laundry.

When the minivan is full of trash, you do the next thing of grabbing a plastic grocery bag (anybody else have a drawer full of them for chores like this?) and filling it with rubbish.

Elliot borrowed inspiration for the phrase from an anonymous Old Saxon poem, which included an archaic spelling of those four simple words as the concluding refrain of each stanza.

The following lines from the poem grabbed my attention especially:

> Do it immediately, do it with prayer;
> Do it reliantly, casting all care;
> Do it with reverence, tracing His hand
> Who placed it before thee with earnest command.
> Stayed on Omnipotence, safe 'neath His wing,
> Leave all results, *do the next thing.*[1]

Shivers of conviction ran down my spine the first time I read these words, which ring just as true for the modern woman as they did for our counterparts many hundreds of years ago—women who would surely have had many more "things" to do next from a purely practical perspective.

Imagine if "do the next thing" included laundry beaten out by hand against a stone rather than tossed into a machine.

Or what if "do the next thing" involved going out to butcher a chicken before dinner could be made?

I will receive protests from current-day mothers who assert that we parent at a much faster pace and with a different set of demands on our time and energy.

I concur. But I also know (from experience) so many of the tasks that intimidate us do so because we have allowed relatively straightforward-but-onerous jobs to pile up, untended, until they have become a mountain we convince ourselves we could never possibly climb, though they started as mere molehills of daily diligence.

Honesty Helps

Once, as I helped clean and organize a house in preparation for the owners to move out, I pushed open the laundry door with great effort to discover what had blocked my entrance: at least three weeks' worth of dirty clothes for a family of eight.

The lady of the house entered behind me, looked around in dismay, and said, "I have no idea how this room looks like this, since all I do is laundry every day. I swear this was all done a few days ago."

The circumstances might not be the same, but I could relate to the ability to hold a different narrative in my mind about my own efficiency than what reality currently reflects. The back patio of our home often suffers neglect because, though I would prefer it to be beautiful and well kept, I tell myself I do not have time to keep it so, rather than taking fifteen minutes each day to tidy the pillows, wipe down the table, water the potted plants, or blow off the leaves.

When we are snowed under by life's demands, we often think about the things we must do more than we do them. And when we've grown weary of doing good, all this pondering and dreading makes us much more tired than motivated.

The result? A dishonest account of why we are where we are.

We tell ourselves we have not ordered supplies for a project because we have been much too diligent in other areas, when the fact is we've ended our day scrolling our phones because we just didn't feel like devoting that energy to ordering the items instead.

Proverbs 22:13 puts it like this: "The sluggard says, 'There is a lion outside! I shall be killed in the streets!'" In other words, we are all capable of claiming the most outlandish reasons for our current struggles in an attempt to avoid responsibility.

I'm not calling you a sluggard, friend. I don't know your life or its demands. But Proverbs contains numerous similar warnings against lying to ourselves about the real reasons we don't complete our tasks or follow through on a promise.

Sometimes the answer is an honest "I did the best I could with the time I had, and there were not enough hours in the day to get to everything. I'll start again tomorrow."

And sometimes the answer is "I procrastinated and avoided because I feel overwhelmed."

When this is the case, honesty, though repugnant at first, becomes a faithful friend that pushes us toward change.

Honesty, though repugnant at first, becomes a faithful friend that pushes us toward change.

Expect Transformation

One of the best parts of my job as an author and a social media "influencer" (a term I usually shy away from but embrace in this instance) is receiving messages like the one below from my friend Kat, a pastor's wife and mom of four. I found Kat through a viral video she posted to the internet in which she did a funny and endearing bit about a particularly relatable aspect of being a mom of small children.

Turns out, she had read *M Is for Mama*, and when she saw me tagging her and "influencing" (there's that word again) others to check out her account, she messaged me the following (which I share with permission): "I always swore I would tell you this if I ever got the chance. My Instagram handle used to be 'mediocre momming 101,' and I made many jokes about mediocre motherhood, annnnnd then I found your book—and promptly dumped all of that. Your book literally changed so much for me, and I praise the Lord for you and the work He is doing through you."

If you're rolling your eyes and thinking, "Well, of course you love this part of your job, Abbie—people are complimenting you," let me assure you, while the "attagirls" are nice, they're not what gets me excited.

Instead, it's the bit that says, "After I read your book, my life changed."

I don't believe for a moment any of my books are necessary for change in a mom's life. The Lord is gracious and faithful to use whatever means He pleases to get our attention. But when He allows something He's prompted me to write to play a part in bringing about "conviction and encouragement" (the two most commonly paired words I've heard to describe both my previous books)—well, that just makes this mama's heart *sing*.

What a privilege to get to partner with the Holy Spirit in exhorting and edifying other moms through God's Word, which never changes and never fails to impact us if only we will receive it honestly and earnestly.

Probably my most favorite feedback of all is something I've received in dozens of messages and in-person conversations at speaking events: "I didn't used to enjoy my kids. But after reading your books, I started spending time in God's Word, unfollowing snarky accounts, retraining my thoughts and mindset, and choosing to look for joy instead of disappointment. And you know what? I'm a completely different mom. I look *forward* to spending time with my kids. They are such a blessing to me."

I blink back tears every time I get to experience the soul-deep joy of picturing these transformed, Spirit-led moms loving on their children from a place of renewed energy and purpose.

Why do I share all this? Because if you're reading this chapter and thinking, "This is all well and good, but how does it materially affect the circumstances I find myself resenting most?" then my answer is "It might not at all."

It's true. And I would be dishonest to imply otherwise.

I cannot guarantee your mother-in-law will be more supportive or the care of your special-needs child will be less demanding or your husband will work fewer hours.

What I can promise you is this: God is not even a little bit surprised by your difficult circumstances but is actively working them together for good for those who love Him and are called according to His purpose (Romans 8:28).

God is not even a little bit surprised by your difficult circumstances but is actively working them together for good for those who love Him and are called according to His purpose.

If that's you, this is *hopeful* news! Not only that, but I promise you the process of surrendering your overwhelm to the Lord, praising Him in *all* circumstances, expecting hard things (and then tackling them in His strength), doing the next thing, and being honest with yourself about your struggles will change your life.

I'm not one to encourage you to follow formulas, but I know the principles found in God's Word are life-altering, and when we apply them faithfully, our thought patterns and actions will evolve into closer alignment with what Philippians 2:5-8 (NKJV) describes as the mind "which was also in Christ Jesus"—a mind saturated with humility and a self-forgetful willingness to obey God, even to the point of death on a cross.

In other words, even though situations you cannot control may stay the same, the circumstances affected most by our attitudes and perspectives—like whether or not we enjoy our children—might very well be altered completely.

Because we're not here simply to expound theory and theology.

We are here to allow these precepts to transform us from a grubby caterpillar into a glorious butterfly.

Certainly, the process will not always be easy or enjoyable.

Did you know, to become a butterfly, a caterpillar must first digest itself? In a gruesome process, the caterpillar releases enzymes inside its chrysalis that dissolve all its tissues into an amorphous goop, and the only elements that remain intact are building blocks called "imaginal disks" necessary for reforming its future self. These imaginal disks (which will become essential body parts such as wings, eyes, legs, and antennae) are present as early as its development inside its egg. As the only components that survive the disintegration of its former self, these disks, fueled by the protein-rich "soup" in which they marinate, eventually reconstitute themselves into the finished product that we recognize as one of God's most breathtaking creatures.[2]

To boil all of this down to its essentials: Change is messy. And painful sometimes. And confusing, as we can't seem to envision how the Lord could possibly take our shambles of a life and rearrange it into something that brings Him glory.

But, man, is it magnificent when at last we emerge, blinking and squinting, into the sunshine of His grace and goodness in our lives, finally grasping the truth that it's been there all along.

A Titus Two Perspective

SUSAN MIDDLETON

mother of nine

I was forty-seven years old. Our youngest child would be starting in our homeschool co-op the following year, finally freeing up that one day a week for a much-needed break. I had so many plans for that time: tennis lessons, a new running plan, volunteering at a local pregnancy center, coffee with friends...on and on; you get the idea. It had taken me quite a while to make it to that point. My husband and I had eight children, and I had been homeschooling for seventeen years. With our last child about to enter kindergarten, it felt like a milestone to be celebrated: the beginning of the end of our homeschooling journey.

Then a positive pregnancy test changed those plans. All of a sudden, my plans were turned upside down. With a baby due just before my forty-eighth birthday, I was forced to confront this question in my heart: Would I be willing to hold my plans and expectations with an open palm? Could I be open to what God sovereignly placed in my life—knowing that it is for my good and His glory? Because of my belief from Scripture that children are a blessing from the Lord, my answer had to be a resounding yes.

Our precious ninth child, Drew, was born just fifteen days before I turned forty-eight. He is such a blessing to our family and reminds us daily that God's plans are better than our own. Even knowing God's plans are better doesn't mean everything is seamless. There are times when I've engaged in pity parties, enviously comparing myself to others my age. On one occasion (okay, probably more than one), I found myself whining to my husband about not fitting in anywhere since I have a baby, two college students, and many ages in between. He graciously responded that I fit in everywhere for that same reason. I could relate to the nursing mom waking up multiple times at night, to the mom dealing with a young child's disobedience, to the mom of a self-centered teen, and to the mom cultivating a relationship with her adult child.

Elisabeth Elliot said, "The secret is Christ in me, not me in a different set of circumstances."[3] Life is not meant to be full of comfort and ease. It is meant to be a life of surrender to the Lord, giving thanks in all circumstances, accepting God's good and perfect will (1 Thessalonians 5:18). My prayer for myself is that I would not grow weary of doing good (Galatians 6:9) and that I would continue to daily love and serve my family with joy and thanksgiving.

I had to smile the other day as I was riding with my ten-year-old son on his go-cart in the rain (just before it ran out of gas). My twenty-five-year-old self would never have imagined this for myself at fifty-eight, but I've learned God's plans are always greater than my own. As I surrender to His plans for my life, I am released from selfishness and the need to be in control. I can rest in His sovereign will, knowing He is working all things together for my good and His glory.

The Narrative

A WORLDLY RESPONSE TO "WORTH IT"	A BIBLICAL RESPONSE TO "WORTH IT"
Thinks the negative way she feels when parenting is hard should inform her actions	Knows her emotions during tough times often amplify the difficulty of her circumstances
Makes excuses for habits that aren't serving her family well	Takes responsibility for areas of improvement
Believes she's too far gone for change	Trusts that God can and will transform her heart and actions as she seeks His will

Action Steps

- Memorize and meditate on Galatians 6:9: "Let us not grow weary of doing good, for in due season we will reap, if we do not give up."
- Choose two things that make you feel "weary of doing good" (meal planning, toddler discipline, bedtime routines, teen dating boundaries, etc.) and pray about/brainstorm ways to address them in a God-honoring way.
- Ask a friend to hold you accountable over the next month to implement the solution to one of these areas the Lord brought to mind.

Questions

Has there been a time in your parenting career when you've felt "weary of doing good"? If so, what did that season look like?

If that period is now, what are some practical steps you could take to alleviate some of your overwhelm?

What is the "next thing" you'd rather not do but know you should?

Prayer

Jesus, You are the ultimate example of obedience to the Father, even unto death. Grant us the strength to welcome opportunities to share in Your sufferings in the everyday struggles of parenting. And may we set our sights on the joy set before us as we persevere. Amen.

CHAPTER 12

Parenting Philosophies That Aren't Worth It

I'm a label avoider—a sometimes unfortunate trait, given the nature of my presence on social media where I receive constant questions like these:

- "What word would you use to classify your homeschooling style?"
- "What denomination do you most align with?"
- "How would you describe your decorating style in one word?"
- "What discipline style in parenting do you use?"

Each of these queries makes me squirm with the discomfort of being *that girl* who isn't even a bit confused about why she homeschools but prefers not to pigeonhole herself into a particular educational lane. Just let me read living books and have my children narrate them *a la* Charlotte Mason right alongside a good old math worksheet and a dash of *Teach Your Child to Read in 100 Easy Lessons*, thank you very much.

Same goes for theology, decorating, writing, and even exercising.

I know who I am and what I believe. But an essential part of "who I am" means I prefer to pick and choose elements that work for me and my family from a variety of biblically sound philosophies and methods.

I've found many kindred spirits in this approach. Very few of us are "one and done" with every area of our lives. But I've also discovered the counterpart to my personality is the label lover. Once this person finds a philosophy that aligns with her lived experience or expectations or emotions, she is all in. I've often heard it described as a feeling of "coming home."

As with just about everything, both approaches come with strengths and weaknesses. For the label avoider, the ability to critically think about an issue without an emotional attachment to the influence of "the group" is a positive, but it's easy to fall into a rebellious mindset of refusing to "go along," even if what you'd be going along with were righteous and good. And for the label lover, the loyalty and dedication are strong, but so is the temptation to make a particular philosophy her identity, to the exclusion of honestly assessing its merits or pitfalls.

Interestingly, regardless of where we fall with either of these camps (and yes, I'm aware of the irony of labeling myself a "label avoider"), we usually prefer other people to define their terms and make it clear where they stand on issues.

Are you an Arminian or a Calvinist?

Are you into this political party or that one?

Are you an authoritarian parent or an authoritative one?

That last question leads us right into a discussion with which it is crucial to engage if we desire to definitively solve the conundrum of how worthwhile (or not) our efforts in motherhood are when all is said, done, said again, redone, swept up, wiped down, and put to bed for the night.

Because the truth is that certain parenting philosophies simply cannot deliver on their claims. And since some have compelling arguments, testimonies, and loyal followings, it's essential we scrutinize every assertion using discernment that comes from the Lord and a knowledge of His Word.

A quote that most attribute to Charles Spurgeon, although I was unable to verify its exact provenance, succinctly sums up the struggle: "Discernment is not the ability to tell the difference between right and wrong; rather, it is telling the difference between right and almost right."

This subtle distinction has tripped up many a Bible-believing parent who just wants to produce God-fearing kids who are well adjusted, kind, and contributing members of society.

Did you catch the problem with that last sentence?

If we "just want to produce" any kind of kid more than we want to obey the God-given mandate to faithfully teach His ways to our children and leave the outcome up to Him, then we will be easy prey for parenting philosophies that promise big results but often yield more heartache than hope.

In the end, any parenting principle that promises "If you'll only follow this formula, you *will* receive this kind of child or have this kind of relationship in return" is biblically unsound. Worse, we might find ourselves worshipping the philosophy rather than the One who gave us the very minds with which we engage with ideas and belief systems. Not only that, but we are flirting with resentment toward God if we aren't awarded an ideal child at the end of all our efforts.

I want to address this phenomenon from two different ends of a pendulum swing in the last fifty years of our culture, and the first example that comes to mind is parenting that is steeped in legalism.

Testing the Spirits

I grew up in East Texas about an hour from Bill Gothard's ALERT Academy, a military-style school whose self-described goal is to "create men who are spiritually sound, physically fit, and ready to serve."[1]

Gothard, for those unfamiliar, is an unmarried evangelist, speaker, and writer whose Institute in Basic Life Principles (IBLP) conferences packed out auditoriums and significantly influenced the homeschooling communities of the '80s, '90s, and early '00s.

Given the fact that my brother and I were homeschooled, coupled with our proximity to the facility, it's no surprise we attended a few IBLP seminars. I mostly remember Gothard's soft-spoken style as he illustrated a particular point from a Bible story through the aid of chalk drawings. (Well, that and his insistence that music with a backbeat is ungodly and a gateway to demonic activity in one's life. No, I'm not kidding.) Beyond that, our family was never involved in anything to do with his organization.

Part of this was due to the fact that my perpetually bearded father refused to abide by Gothard's clean-shaven policy—just one of several rigid rules for personal appearance required for participation in any of IBLP's advanced training programs.

Other things that disqualified us? A propensity for wearing shorts, listening to Christian rock music, and watching select movies and TV shows.

In other words, despite the fact my parents were considered too conservative by most of their secular peers (and even quite a few Christian ones), we were not "up to snuff" for IBLP.

In recent years, Gothard and his various ministries have come under fire due to a variety of allegations ranging from cultish, controlling behavior to sexual harassment and misconduct. While this chapter is in no way an attempt to confirm or deny any of the specifics of such claims—although Gothard did step down as the head of IBLP in 2014 in the wake of these accusations[2]—I personally know enough families who were pulled in by the magnetic promise of "results" to attest to the dysfunction (and sometimes downright devastation) that lies on the other side of unquestioning adherence to the predetermined life path IBLP championed.

What I want to make clear is that, while IBLP (or a similar organization called Vision Forum, whose leader, Doug Phillips, also stepped down due to sexually inappropriate behavior[3]) will likely be the primary entity that comes to mind for many reading this book, they are hardly the only ones. When I describe the downfalls of parenting from a place of legalism or religiosity, a guarantee of a particular outcome if only we will dress a certain way, wear our hair a certain way, speak a certain way, view only certain forms of media, and associate with only certain social circles is hardly unique to a few men or organizations.

We see these tendencies in many "closed communities" (think any group—religious, ethnic, ideological, or otherwise—into which entry is difficult due to a long list of strictures or guidelines). And we must always be diligent to compare every claim to the truth of God's Word. We cannot "believe every spirit, but test the spirits to see whether they are from God, for many false prophets have gone out into the world" (1 John 4:1).

Principles, Not Prescriptions

Of course, rampant biblical illiteracy and a desire to be spoon-fed a case-by-case game plan hampers many believers from testing much of anything against the Bible. Based on the number of messages I receive asking for a formula (whether they explicitly use the word or not) for locked-down results on everything from discipline and potty training to teen attitudes, dating, and grocery shopping (you wouldn't believe the number of questions I receive about the appropriate amount and methods of allowing snacking) to memorizing Bible verses and homeschooling (shall I go on, or do you get the point?), I'd say we humans like our "recipes for success."

The problem is if I tell you, "The only right way to potty train is to start at two, run around stark naked (the child, not you) for one full week, drink copious clear liquids, and spend every possible waking moment in the bathroom," and *it doesn't work*, you're going to be pretty disillusioned with the hoops I've made you jump through only to end the week cranky and exhausted with a child who still poops his pants.

By contrast, if I tell you, "I might wait until they show interest. When they do, be consistent to take them often. Encourage them when they do well. Be patient. They might do it quickly, or you may have to work on it for a while. But they won't still be peeing in their undies when they're a teenager," you might walk away with *principles* that are true for most parents and children (special needs excepted), while feeling empowered that you have freedom to use discernment for each of your individual children and tailor the potty-training experience to his or her particular needs.

Thankfully, we have been given freedom in Christ to pursue a variety of biblically solid approaches to each of the topics (and so many more) for which I just mentioned I often get "formula requests."

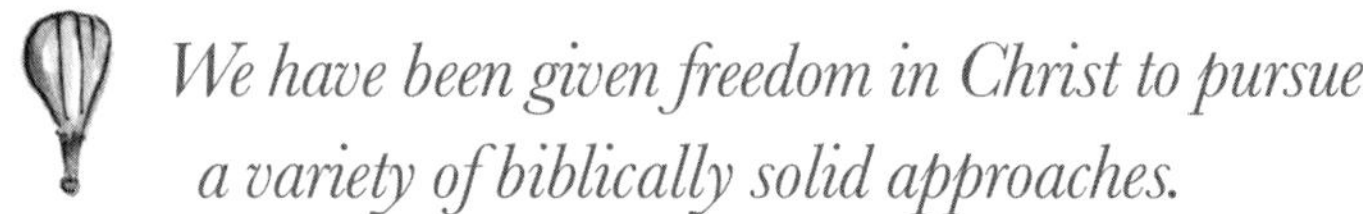

In truth, many of the legalistic movements associated with Christianity at the end of the twentieth century were reactions to the hedonistic, drug-fueled experimentation of the sexual revolution in the '60s and '70s (which, come to think of it, was also a type of formula—promising freedom, pleasure, and autonomy without consequence to those who abandoned traditional Judeo-Christian values).

A Pendulum Swing

Not surprisingly, when one movement begins to show its rotten fruit, the pendulum of opinion will inevitably swing toward a polarized approach, which is exactly what we're seeing with the rise in philosophies like "gentle parenting," "conscious parenting," and "peaceful parenting" among secular and Christian parents alike.

All three versions (and any similar variety I've omitted) promise parents a better way to connect with their children. A better way to engage with conflict. A better way to process emotions. A better way to *live*.

If you're unfamiliar with the tenets of gentle parenting, a term coined by British author Sarah Ockwell-Smith in her 2016 text *The Gentle Parenting Book*, the label alone might cause you to wonder what objections I could possibly have.

After all, gentleness is listed as a fruit of the Spirit in Galatians 5:22-23. Ephesians 4:2 (NIV) exhorts us to be "completely humble and gentle; be patient, bearing with one another in love." And in Matthew 11:29, Jesus describes Himself as "gentle and lowly in heart."

Clearly, a precedent exists throughout Scripture for gentleness, patience, and compassion toward others, a standard that should naturally include our own children, as we strive to convey the care and forbearance of a heavenly Father who loved us enough to send His own Son as a substitutionary atonement for our own sin.

Ah, but I've already arrived at a snag between (1) gentle parenting as a secular philosophy, which seeks to move parents away from the pitfalls of authoritarian, my-way-or-the-highway tyranny toward a view of parenting as "life coaching," and (2) a biblical view of gentleness, which will always align with the truth of our need for a Savior.

Not One Righteous

One of the bedrock beliefs of gentle parenting is that human beings are basically good. In fact, one of the largest gentle parenting accounts, boasting millions of followers, has the tagline "good inside" in her handle.

In one post from this account, the author soothes her readers with this idea: It's okay if putting myself first feels uncomfortable. Discomfort is a sign of doing something new, not something wrong. My needs matter.

This theme of nothing and no one ever being classified as "wrong" persists across every secular iteration of the philosophy that I have encountered. Yet that teaching is patently, biblically inaccurate, since Romans 3:10 assures us, "None is righteous, no, not one." (That includes our kids, y'all.)

It should be enough to ward off any Christian parent, and yet more and more Christian moms, especially, are gravitating toward the allure of a parenting philosophy that promises peace and connection.

The thing is, the post I just shared contains a mixture of half-truths and outright lies. Yes, our needs do matter, and Matthew 7:11 validates this in a decidedly ungentle parenting way by saying, "If you then, who are evil, know how to give good gifts to your children, how much more will your Father who is in heaven give good things to those who ask him!" After describing God's care for the wildflowers and the sparrows, Matthew 10:31 concludes not with "So be sure to put yourself first, guilt-free" but with "Fear not, therefore; you are of more value than many sparrows."

But also? There is such a thing as right and wrong. And sometimes putting yourself first is wrong. If you're mad that I said it's wrong, please read on for what the Bible has to say. And if you're bristling that I only said "sometimes," there are times when it's wise to eat first before you feed the baby so you can have fuel for milk and a better mental state when the toddler inevitably knocks to the kitchen floor the plate of food meant to keep him occupied.

So, what *does* the Bible have to say about putting yourself first as a general rule?

We've touched on these passages previously, but it bears repeating that Jesus, after describing the sacrifices inherent to the Christian life, says, "Many who are first will be last, and the last first" (Matthew 19:30).

He also exhorts us, "If anyone wants to come after Me, he must deny himself, take up his cross daily, and follow Me" (Luke 9:23 NASB).

And Paul underscores the point with Philippians 2:3, which says, "In humility count others more significant than yourselves."

Examining Every Philosophy of Man

Not every tenet of gentle parenting clashes with biblical wisdom. A general focus on respect for everyone, including children, and emotional self-regulation jibes well with numerous biblical exhortations to "love one another" (John 13:34), to exercise self-control (2 Timothy 1:7), and to treat each other with consideration as image-bearers (Philippians 2:4).

But other questionable precepts have little to no support from Scripture, with an emphasis on the following guidelines (which emerge as consistent themes in gentle parenting podcasts, books, articles, and social media posts):

- All emotions are valid and worthy of attention.
- Both punishment and reward are off-limits.
- Empathy is king.
- Children should question any and all authority.
- Undesirable behavior results from developmental limitations, from feeling "unsafe," or from deficiency in care, never from one's own sinful tendencies.

(If you adhere to one of the parenting styles I've mentioned and disagree with any part of this list, please understand it's compiled from sifting through the many and varied components that fall under the umbrella of "gentle parenting."

As with any philosophy, a wide variety of both beliefs and practice tend to get crowded under one label, and not every practitioner will agree.)

This is a chapter about the fact that philosophies that promise us "results" more than they encourage us to trust the Giver of all good gifts are not worth our while.

So, what does gentle parenting promise us?

The Gentle Parenting Book boasts the tagline "How to Raise Calmer, Happier Children from Birth to Seven." And a similarly themed book called *Raising Good Humans* has the subtitle "A Mindful Guide to Breaking the Cycle of Reactive Parenting and Raising Kind, Confident Kids."

Sounds great, doesn't it?

Understandably, many a survivor of "reactive parenting," which often manifests in shouting, harsh punishment, and out-of-control emotions, has welcomed both the formula and the promised outcome of gentle parenting with open arms.

In fact, more than a few former members of groups like IBLP have happily ridden the pendulum swing from the rigid rules of their youth all the way over to the realm of "reparenting my inner child" and "holding space for every emotion," convinced there can be no downside to such ideas as long as they represent an abrupt about-face from their own upbringing.

The irony? Many legalistic parents were trying to undo the damage inflicted by lax and neglectful parents who were more concerned with pursuing pleasure than investing in the next generation.

Each new version vows to repair the damage of the past.

The problems come when not enough people "hold space" for an honest examination of whether yet another parenting theory that assures us of a particular payoff actually aligns with God's Word. Regardless of a particular parenting style's origins (but especially if spawned from secular ideologies), we should be Bereans, "examining the Scriptures daily to see whether these things [are] so" (Acts 17:11), comparing every philosophy of man to biblical truth.

Not only that, but when proponents of an ideology ban even mild dissenters, discourage questions and critical thinking, and respond with aggression and sarcasm when challenged, alarm bells should be ringing.

Aggressively "Right"

Once, following my guest appearance on a podcast called *The Spillover*, during which I discussed some biblical concerns with gentle parenting, I received two separate messages from readers who'd been kicked out of two distinct "crunchy Christian moms" Facebook groups for mentioning the podcast and my name.

At first, I assumed I'd misunderstood some context. My manner on the podcast was far from contentious. Surely, a mere reference to someone who had concerns about a parenting philosophy could not prompt such a response.

But then one of the readers explained that the administrator of one page, herself a proponent for and longtime practitioner of gentle parenting, had asked for advice about curbing disrespectful behavior and abusive speech (toward her and each other) in her preteens and teens. When members expressed objections to gentle parenting, she blocked them, and when my reader suggested she check out my thoughts on the podcast, the admin responded with "Oh, we're well aware of Abbie Halberstadt," and then blocked the reader without further dialog.

It's hardly an isolated incident or one limited to religious pages. When Jessica Winter, a contributor to the *New Yorker*, objected to a prominent gentle parenting advocate's disdainful representation of parents whose spouses (which, in my interactions, always equates to "the fathers") do not gentle parent, she was summarily blocked from the group page.[4]

I've heard from dozens of readers who have told me that "gentle parents must save all their gentleness for their kids because they're the meanest people in comment sections."

And lest you think I'm implying this behavior is limited to gentle parenting groups, I'm fully aware dissenting members of authoritarian parenting groups are threatened with discipline, excommunication, and even eternal damnation.

Neither do the more militant members bother with basic civility, often engaging in debates on gentle parenting pages with petty name-calling and condescension, trading ideological blows in the name of "being right."

On the opposite end of the spectrum from gentle parenting, one reviewer expressed a general appreciation for *M Is for Mama* but called into question my commitment to scriptural truth simply because I had failed to specifically recommend spanking as a primary form of biblical correction (or, in keeping with my practice of promoting principles over prescriptions, make any reference to it at all, for that matter.)

In other words, whenever we find our identity in an allegiance to anything other than Christ first and foremost, we will feel threatened by any criticism, real or perceived, of our beloved belief systems, and any fruit of the Spirit we lay claim to will look like the shriveled-up lemons I sometimes find languishing in the back of my crisper drawer.

Whenever we find our identity in an allegiance to anything other than Christ first and foremost, we will feel threatened by any criticism, real or perceived, of our beloved belief systems, and any fruit of the Spirit we lay claim to will look like the shriveled-up lemons I sometimes find languishing in the back of my crisper drawer.

Our Theology Should Lead Our Practice

I've interacted with thousands of moms who hold the full spectrum of stances on parenting, so I can already hear some of the objections rolling in: "I parent like I do *because* I love Jesus first and foremost, Abbie. We're not Christians in a vacuum. It's going to affect everything we do. So what? Do we just 'love Christ' and never have an opinion about anything?"

Far from it, friends.

I completely agree our devotion to Christ should spill over into every area of our lives. And if we parent, exercise, speak about our neighbors, make dinner, school our children, consume media, interact with other internet users, go to church, and mow our lawns the way we do as a natural overflow of love for Jesus and His Holy Word, chances are we won't be attached to any methodology more than we are to the idea of applying it in a way that honors God.

It's when we get our priorities backward and begin to think about, speak about, and act on our philosophies more than we read our Bibles, ask God for wisdom in prayer, and discuss things with our own spouses (instead of telling our husbands to "do better" or get in line with what our Facebook group said) that things get dicey.

Even dicier is when we start twisting Scripture to fit our own parenting narrative.

Jinger Vuolo, in *Becoming Free Indeed*, a book that focuses on her journey away from a legalistic upbringing in IBLP and toward a genuine love for Christ, says, "If a teacher says the Christian life can only be lived successfully with some secret bit of knowledge they have discovered, then that teacher should be avoided at all costs."

To a great extent, I agree. God's Word is available and applicable to every Christian. Every teaching and claim of man should be thoroughly examined by its "lamp" (Psalm 119:105) with an "eat the meat, spit out the bones" approach that allows us to spot the tidbits of goodness, if any, amidst the treacherous parts that have the potential to harm us long after we swallow them whole. Sometimes there won't be enough good to bother with the rest of the mess. Sometimes we'll find value in the parts that align scripturally while letting the rest go.

The Gospel Coalition took this approach in an article entitled "Is 'Gentle Parenting' Biblical?" which conceded that if it were "just a mood board for solving parenting difficulties in nonconfrontational ways, I'd have nothing to say against it."[5]

But, since gentle parenting denies sin nature and advocates for zero punishment or reward, the author could not fully back the philosophy (and did an admirable job of supporting his objections with an exegetically thorough examination of God's Word on both topics).

If you're wondering why it matters whether we teach our kids about sin, punishment, and reward, a post I stumbled upon in a gentle parenting Facebook thread underscores the importance of a living, breathing, biblically sound theology that impacts everything we do.

The crux of the post was one woman's cry for help from other moms in the group. The problem? This mom, a self-proclaimed gentle parent, could not figure out how to explain a biblically accurate accounting of Resurrection Sunday without acknowledging that Jesus had died on the cross for our sins.

Isaiah 53:5 (NASB) says, "He was pierced for our offenses, He was crushed for our wrongdoings; the punishment for our well-being was laid upon Him, and by His wounds we are healed."

"He was pierced for our offenses,
He was crushed for our wrongdoings;
the punishment for our well-being was
laid upon Him, and by His wounds
we are healed" (Isaiah 53:5 NASB).

But this mom could not share even an age-appropriate paraphrase of this powerful, hope-filled truth with her child, because her gentle parenting ideologies prohibited her from ever punishing him in any way or even reprimanding any of his behavior. In other words, the idea of the consequences Jesus bore for our sake was completely foreign (and abhorrent) to him.

In a true agony of indecision, she acknowledged her parenting choices were hamstringing her ability to preach the gospel to her son, who became very distraught at even the suggestion of wrongdoing or Jesus's death. She could not bring herself to abandon her philosophies, and so she found herself questioning her faith instead.

The solution one member of the group suggested to reconcile the two was simply to reframe Jesus's death as "something he and God agreed he needed to do to make people who were used to offering animal sacrifices feel better so they could understand they were already good and accepted by God."

Not only is this viewpoint found nowhere in Scripture or any creeds of historical Christianity for the last 2,000 years, but it runs in direct opposition to Romans 1:16, which declares, "I am not ashamed of the gospel, for it is the power of God for salvation to everyone who believes."

Correction, Consequences, Discipline, and Reward

In an interview on the *Ellen Fisher Podcast*, during which I was invited to engage with a clinical psychologist on the topic of opposing parenting philosophies, I found myself fascinated to encounter a worldview that borrowed heavily from Judeo-Christian values while painting a layer of agnostic pragmatism on top of any problematic areas.

I agreed with Dr. Laura Markham, a self-labeled "peaceful parent," on many topics—from holding boundaries to acknowledging emotions without valorizing or enshrining them as primary decision-makers to teaching respect to and requiring it from children from an early age.

Truthfully, her commonsense stances were refreshingly actionable compared to the convoluted role-playing and game-centered efforts to counter problematic behavior I've encountered on many gentle parenting accounts.

Significant sticking points, though?

Correction, consequences, discipline, and reward.

Hebrews 11:6 (BSB) assures us "anyone who approaches [God] must believe that He exists and that He rewards those who earnestly seek Him."

Matthew 6:3-4 says, "But when you give to the needy, do not let your left hand know what your right hand is doing...And your Father who sees in secret will reward you."

Hebrews 12:7 points out "it is for discipline that you have to endure. God is treating you as sons. For what son is there whom his father does not discipline?" And then, in verses 10-11, the author drives the point home: "[God] disciplines us for our good, so that we may share His holiness. All discipline for the moment seems not to be joyful, but sorrowful; yet to those who have been trained by it, afterwards it yields the peaceful fruit of righteousness" (NASB 1995).

I could go on with many more positive references to correction, consequences, discipline, and reward in the Bible, but these brief examples stand in stark contrast to Dr. Markham's claims that every form of punishment negatively affects our children by breaking our connection to them.

Interestingly, when I described a consequence we might apply to a teen who wanted to attend a social event but had not cleaned his room, she responded with "I would call that structure, not punishment."

The same tweaked definition applied to her requiring a child to leave a sandbox if she threw sand and taking away access to flashlights in bed and chocolate if indulged in without permission.

When I pointed out children often perceive as punishment anything that hinders their wishes being fulfilled, she insisted that, as long as connection to our children is maintained (presumably, in this case, by calling it something other than punishment) or repaired correctly (according to an accepted protocol set by clinical standards), we *would* experience peace in our homes and enjoy the respect and cooperation of our children. (Did you catch the formula there?)

Rather than using terms like "right" or "wrong," Dr. Markham called this happy state of connection and reciprocal cooperation "choosing love." She explained that because her daughter wanted to keep the connection with her mom strong, she made sure to "choose love" by showing up on time for curfew, making good grades, and refusing temptation when a friend suggested they sneak out during a sleepover. As a result, Dr. Markham said, she'd never once had to reprimand her child or even raise her voice.

Connection Does Not Equal Control

This theme of establishing and nurturing connection or relationship to our children as a means of achieving our parenting ends undergirds many of the online posts I've encountered in my reading—posts that stand in defiance to upbringings that prioritized immediate obedience over mutual respect or even basic consideration for development limitations or circumstantial struggles.

One particular post told the story of a teenager who failed to pick up a sibling after a music practice. That afternoon, the mother said, she avoided all references to discipline or consequences, greeting her child with a hug instead and wheedling her with "*Somebody* didn't pick up her sister, which worried *somebody's* mom. Can *somebody* tell me more about this?"

While I didn't love this approach, which struck me as condescending and unnecessarily roundabout, I completely agreed with her decision to withhold punishment in favor of a conversation in this instance. According to the poster, her daughter was usually conscientious, and this behavior was out of the ordinary. She pointed out how her leniency kept the lines of communication open and corrected the behavior for the future with no punishment necessary. And then she promised her readers they never need give their children consequences again.

Curious, I headed to the comments and immediately encountered what I expected: parents who needed to know how to apply this approach to children who *were* repeat offenders, did not respond well to playful conversations, and were currently throwing up both middle fingers to all their parents' requests.

The poster went from one frustrated reader to another, assuring them of the same thing: If they would only establish a genuine connection with their child, they *would* see the results they craved. In other words, the only reason their children were *not* falling in line was because they had failed to nurture their relationship well (or, at least, well enough).

Friends, I know from personal experience (and God's Word) this is no more true than "If you follow these five exclusive-to-our-group rules for purity and righteousness, you'll get the results you crave" or even "If you read the Bible every day, limit your children's access to phones, carefully screen their friend groups, love them unconditionally, take them on one-on-one dates, always apologize when you mess up, and are never too strict or too lax, you'll get the results you crave."

THE LORD HAS
SO MUCH BETTER
PLANNED FOR
YOU THAN
PARENTING
SLAVERY
TO ANY
IDEOLOGY.

Faith Over Formulas

Formulaic parenting that elevates its principles above biblical truth makes big promises, but it delivers bondage. If you think I'm being dramatic, I could tell you story after story of panicked parents enslaved to lists of pharisaical dos and don'ts, worried if they loosen up on even one, their kids won't "turn out okay." I could also regale you with tales of moms terrified they will traumatize their children for life if they fail to self-regulate, establish and hold certain boundaries (without the benefit of consequences if they're crossed), and listen with empathy while validating every emotion.

It's exhausting. It's defeating. And it's unbiblical.

Instead of assurances of guaranteed results, the best encouragement I can give stressed-out parents is this: "For freedom Christ has set us free; stand firm therefore, and do not submit again to a yoke of slavery" (Galatians 5:1).

"For freedom Christ has set us free; stand firm therefore, and do not submit again to a yoke of slavery" (Galatians 5:1).

The Lord calls us to something so much better than parenting slavery to any ideology, whether one of rigid rules or psychological hoop jumping.

Step into this truth with confidence that Christ will equip you, grow you, and *stretch* you to the max—because He loves you too much to leave you in a cage of your own making.

A Titus Two Perspective

GINGER HUBBARD

author, speaker, podcast host, mom of two, stepmom of two

Today's culture seems to be more focused on the feelings of children than their spiritual welfare. Helping children process and navigate difficult emotions in healthy ways is important. However, anti-discipline trends that claim to be "grace based" have parents sacrificing opportunities to help children recognize their sins and turn to Jesus for rescue on the altar of coddling sinful responses to emotions. Yet, the Bible teaches that discipline and grace are not mutually exclusive.

We know from Proverbs 3:12 that "the LORD disciplines those he loves" (NIV). Our gracious heavenly Father desires His children to live in the blessings, promises, and safety of His will. Consequences are part of God's merciful plan to redirect the paths of His children for their good and His glory, which is why He commands parents, "Do not withhold discipline from a child" (Proverbs 23:13 NIV).

When children are trained and disciplined in the ways of the Lord, which involves requiring them to live self-controlled lives and obey parental authority, it has a positive effect on their emotional state. Consider children who lack discipline and self-control. Are they happy, satisfied children with healthy emotions, or are they unhappy, unsatisfied children who've become slaves to their emotions? Are they joyful and content, or are they whiny and demanding? Are they enjoying life, or do they seem miserable most of the time—especially when they aren't getting their way?

Parents do children no favors by excusing disobedience under the guise of being gentle or showing grace. The neglect of discipline is not gentle, loving, or grace-based. To the contrary, it enables children to stay on a self-serving path of destruction, endangering their physical, emotional, and spiritual well-being.

Proverbs 13:24 confirms, "Whoever spares the rod hates their children, but the one who loves their children is careful to discipline them" (NIV). Notice the word "careful." Biblical discipline is not an angry, abusive reaction to a child's bad behavior. It's a loving, self-controlled response to their need for wisdom and the transformational power of Christ in their lives.

Biblical discipline teaches children the law of the harvest. When children experience consequences for disobedience, they learn that God has built the principle of sowing and reaping into their lives. This valuable lesson imparts wisdom for daily living, making it one that parents should strive to teach, not avoid. Parents who understand God's holy intentions for discipline will view it through the lens of love and administer it as an act of love.

May our faithfulness to bring our children up in the discipline and instruction of the Lord serve as a beautiful demonstration of His love and grace.

The Narrative

A WORLDLY RESPONSE TO "WORTH IT"	A BIBLICAL RESPONSE TO "WORTH IT"
Relies on formulas for parenting	Puts her trust in the truth of God's Word
Refuses to assess or abandon philosophies that contradict biblical principles	Sets aside any worldly philosophy that goes against the Bible
Trusts in philosophies of man to bring results	Knows the only guaranteed "results" in parenting come in the form of peace in following the will of God

Action Steps

- Memorize and meditate on Galatians 5:1: "For freedom Christ has set us free; stand firm therefore, and do not submit again to a yoke of slavery."
- Make a list of three bedrock parenting principles you live by.
- Examine your own upbringing. Identify strengths and weaknesses in the way you were raised.

Questions

How did you arrive at the foundational parenting principles you listed previously? What scriptural support do you have for each one? Is it consistent throughout the whole Bible or limited to a one-verse support?

Do you feel that you parent from a position of peace or from a position of anxiety? How or why do you feel this way?

If someone questions your parenting, how do you respond? If defensively, where do you feel this reaction comes from?

Prayer

Jesus, thank You that the only "formula" worth paying attention to is "repent and believe." You paid our debt of sin on the cross, and we are free to rest in the completed work of righteousness in every area, including how we parent. Hallelujah, what a Savior!

CHAPTER 13

A Tiger-Striped Soul

Signora. Signora, you must move."

Startled, I lifted my head to see a priest advancing toward me, flapping his hands as if he were shooing away a bug, an expression of disgust on his face.

"Outside. You may feed your child *outside* on the benches. Go. Now." His head wagged side to side in disapproval, and I wondered how I would struggle to my feet while holding a nursing two-year-old.

In a move of desperation, I'd chosen a spot against a wall near a corner in St. Peter's Basilica to plop down on the floor, cover myself with a muslin blanket, and nurse a very distraught twinbie in an attempt to quiet his shrieks, which were reverberating off every polished marble surface, every stoic chiseled statue.

The benches outside the basilica were perpetually crowded, and my primary thought was for silence and sanity for all, not propriety.

Embarrassment flooded my body, a visceral tingling rush, as the priest towered over me, arms folded across the front of his cassock, clearly determined to ensure that I vacated the premises before he walked away. I felt like a child who had been caught stealing from the candy store.

In an adrenaline-fueled feat, I used the wall as leverage to push myself to a standing position, somehow managing not to drop Toby or let the blanket slide to the floor. As I headed for the exit, I sneaked a peek over one shoulder and spotted the priest walking away, back straight, head erect, clearly convinced of a job well done.

Outside, I encountered a crowd of tourists perched on every surface, including multiple able-bodied men and women who stared indifferently at me as I scanned the benches, and Toby arched his back and wailed to nurse. They owed me nothing, but, oh, how I longed for an understanding or sympathetic face in that moment.

My pulse pounded in my temples, and I could hear a roaring sensation in my ears as my cortisol levels steadily climbed to new heights of anxiety. I rushed past more milling onlookers and trotted down the steps, barely keeping Toby from throwing himself onto the stone pavers, scanning frantically for somewhere, anywhere to hide.

But there was nowhere.

So I contented myself with dropping onto the top step of some stairs with no one in sight and went back to the business of nursing my toddler, hopeful he'd return to reason once he'd had his fill. Sixty seconds later, I spotted a guard striding toward us with a steely expression. Gun-shy from my previous encounter with the priest, I jumped up, dislodging Toby and setting off a fresh wave of protests. As I fled to another flight of stairs, on which most of my family members were now sitting, I lost my balance in my haste to descend and stumbled down three steps, barely managing to keep from taking a hard tumble with my toddler in front of fifty day-trippers.

Yet again, there was nowhere to go, nowhere to bury my head in my arms and let fall the tears that clogged my throat and burned the backs of my eyes. I'm not a dramatic person by nature, but my emotions were screaming at me that the previous ten minutes were some of the worst of my life.

I was *done* with traveling with small children, *done* with intolerant, dour priests, *done* with Rome.

I sincerely contemplated putting both twinbies in our double stroller and walking three miles in the sweltering afternoon heat back to the relative cool of our rental just so I wouldn't have to be around people anymore. The revulsion on the priest's face kept coming to my mind, a fresh wave of shame washing over me each time it did.

A Little Kindness Goes a Long Way

As I sat and finally finished nursing Toby, making my body as small and inconspicuous as possible, my pulse began to slow. And a single thought reverberated through my brain again and again: "I shouldn't have sat on the floor. That was obviously offensive to that priest. But what a difference it would have made *if* he had politely approached me and respectfully let me know." (And I suspect, had I encountered a different priest, I would have encountered a more courteous exchange.)

Granted, my rule-following self would probably still have experienced some chagrin at my gaffe. But I wouldn't have felt like a criminal and an outcast. I wouldn't have been tempted to quit and go home right then and there. I wouldn't have wanted the earth to swallow me whole.

It's true there were multiple contributing factors to all the feelings I just described, including too little sleep, exhaustion from being in a constantly rotating environment for the fourth week in a row, and the fact that I couldn't remember the last time we'd gone more than a few hours without a toddler meltdown.

I was tired. And my endurance was wearing thin.

But a little kindness would have gone a long way toward reviving my weary spirit and renewing my mindset from one of defeat to one of hope.

Maybe you can relate?

You're all in with this mothering business, but you keep making mistakes, losing your temper, unintentionally breaking "the rules." And every time you do, it seems like somebody—the internet, your mom, that lady at church who told your toddler to "hush"—is all over your back. And you just feel kind of embarrassed and angry and over it.

I know for a fact I'm describing at least a few of you because you're in my inbox right now.

Do you know the most common question I get on Whaddya Wanna Know Wednesday? It's not about a particular topic. Instead, it always starts with these six words: "Do you have any encouragement for…"

Due to time constraints, my answer can't always be an individualized tidbit for every request, but my general answer is a resounding "YES! I DO!" I've done my best to share it with you time and again throughout this motherhood trilogy I've been privileged to write, echoing Paul's words in Philippians 2:1-2: "So if there is any encouragement in Christ, any comfort from love, any participation in the Spirit, any affection and sympathy, complete my joy by being of the same mind, having the same love, being in full accord and of one mind."

This is the truth and the hope of sisterhood in Christ. When our encouragement, joy, comfort, and purpose come from the same God and Father of us all, we are united across mothering stages, locations, denominations, and circumstances. We can pray for each other, cheer each other on, "stir up one another to love and good works" (Hebrews 10:24), and show compassion on those days when we're all struggling a bit more than usual.

This is the truth and the hope of sisterhood in Christ. When our encouragement, joy, comfort, and purpose come from the same God and Father of us all, we are united across mothering stages, locations, denominations, and circumstances. We can pray for each other, cheer each other on, "stir up one another to love and good works" (Hebrews 10:24), and show compassion on those days when we're all struggling a bit more than usual.

I'm so glad Shaun and my children gathered around me on the steps of St. Peter's Basilica that day as the tears trickled silently down my burning cheeks. I'm so grateful they urged me to stay with the group instead of heading back to the rental with my tail between my legs. I'm so thankful they walked beside me through a hard moment to the other side. If they hadn't, I'd have missed out on a delightful afternoon of sightseeing at the Colosseum, gelatos near Trevi Fountain, and delicious Italian street food for dinner.

And so, here I sit, fervently typing the same encouragement to you, friends.

Stay. Don't retreat in defeat. You don't want to miss out on what comes next. I can't promise you it will be easy, but I can guarantee you the Lord will fight for you in it and through it as you refuse to give up and refuse to back down from the truth that your work matters.

And not just for your own children.

A Generation Adrift

When we boldly grasp hold of the lasting impact our steadfast, imperfect-yet-faithful investment in our families can have, even in the face of the most disdainful and disgusted responses from the world, we embrace at least a tiny sliver of this truth: Your persistence in pouring yourself out "as a living sacrifice" (Romans 12:1) to your family for the sake of Christ has the potential to cause ripple effects of redemption through your community, through your country, and even, hyperbolic though it may sound, through the world.

We shouldn't be surprised since we clearly see the ripples, which sometimes feel like tidal waves, that result from a worldview that grasps at instant pleasures and self-justification.

Once, when I asked readers to share their experiences with teens and young adults who were not their own children in an attempt to gauge the effects of our culture's self-focus on upcoming generations, one mom of young children sent me an account of her experience as a coffee shop franchise owner.

I found her descriptions of the kind of teen and young adult behaviors she and her husband routinely deal with as business owners fascinating in the same way I find it almost impossible to look away from a car wreck as I drive slowly by. But what I appreciated most was the undercurrent of affection she displayed for her young employees, saying that though her own children were under ten years old, "I LOVE the high school and college age group." Far from viewing them as lost causes or mere nuisances, it was clear she thought of them as individuals worthy of respect and consideration, regardless of their misguided behaviors.

Still, I felt my blood pressure rising as she described employees who regularly got high in the bathroom during shifts and made no attempt to hide it, despite the shop's clearly stated policies on substance abuse during work hours.

Curious, I asked her why they wouldn't at least try to disguise their off-limits activities to avoid termination, something my own peers would have done in the same situation twenty years ago.

Her response hit me like a sucker punch: "Subjective truth means the rules don't apply unless [they] want them to. There was no secrecy or covertness, just surprise that the rules are the rules for everyone. It's also destroyed boundaries by keeping right and wrong based on feelings, which makes it really hard to give or receive objective feedback. The concept of hurting someone's feelings has been criminalized. It's hard to give feedback for most people, but when hurting someone's feelings is 'abuse'? That makes you afraid to speak the truth even in kindness."

It brought to mind a quote imprinted on the jean jacket of a young man, dressed from head to toe in Pepto-Bismol pink, in front of me in the Chick-fil-A line one day: "Thank you for standing behind me in all that I do. I hope you are as happy with me as I am with you."

This concept of championing another's life choices, regardless of their morality, practicality, or potentially detrimental impact, has infiltrated everything from books to social media and is now so prevalent we find it printed on clothing. I especially found the part about being "as happy with me as I am with you" unsettling, as it feels a bit like trying to stab pudding with a fork. From one day to the next, how "happy" I feel with another human being might change, depending on my mood, their behavior, or a combination of the two. What a nebulous factor on which to pin any true "hope."

But it aligns perfectly with what my reader learned in her four and a half years managing young adults.

"Feelings and taking care of oneself are top priority," the franchise owner observed. "The concept of needing to take a 'mental health day' has been so normalized and praised. It almost doesn't occur to many that their team needs them. If they are feeling a little down or tired, everything stops. It makes sense this age is a little egocentric, but the scale we've seen is far greater than normal. I think it's due to the culture's simultaneously prioritizing feelings and self."

She also shared that "75 percent of our staff was on some sort of medication for mental health or in therapy, or both. They talk about their anxiety meds with each other like they talk about the weather."

These numbers are certainly higher than the reported national average in the United States but do jibe with multiple statistics I've encountered while doing research for this book that describe a troubling spike in mental health issues among teens and young adults.

The Kids Are Not Okay

Abigail Shrier, in her book *Bad Therapy: Why the Kids Aren't Growing Up*, says that "the rising generation has received more therapy than any prior generations. Nearly *40 percent* of the rising generation has received treatment from a mental health professional" and "forty-two percent of the rising generation currently has a mental health diagnosis, rendering 'normal' increasingly 'abnormal.'"[1]

Despite the phenomenon of increased therapy, she points out that "less than half of Gen Zers believe their mental health is 'good.'" In other words, therapy, while helpful for some patients, does not seem to be the fix-all many health professionals have claimed.

Not only that, but as Shrier declares on Mark Manson's podcast, "We've never had a generation more focused on its feelings and, frankly, not one more tyrannized by their feelings."[2]

It's easy to feel deflated after absorbing all these sobering statistics. But my coffee-shop-owning reader offered an optimistic perspective for every parent choosing to resolutely swim against the current of zero objective standards and constant affirmation, regardless of merit.

"Accountability is their best motivator," she said, acknowledging that every effort they'd made to incentivize their young employees with rewards and competitions failed. "As we were prepping another competition...one of our managers in her mid-twenties straight-up told me that consequences are the only reliable motivator with this generation and that such promotions are a waste. Her statement only confirmed my private thoughts from years prior. [These kids] are not hungry, but instead overfull. With the poke of accountability, you would see instant change. They desperately want clear boundaries, even though they struggle with feedback. The bummer is it's much less fun to give a write-up than to throw a pizza party."

(It's a particularly fascinating insight in light of our discussion in the last chapter on parenting philosophies that advocate for the eradication of consequences.)

She finished up, however, with this buoyant note: "So many of these high school and college kids are OPEN and want to figure out what is right and wrong. They are so fun to accomplish things with, and they love to be partnered with in a way that allows them responsibility. They need concrete (Jesus!) under their feet, instead of shifting sands from culture."

Plant Dads and Dog Moms

Friends, we have the opportunity, daunting though it may seem at times, to engage with a culture hungry for Truth, even while they declare it doesn't exist. And one of the best ways we can do this is by equipping our own children with the kind of solid biblical foundation that will never crack or cave to cultural pressure.

I've been careful to point out that though the foundation of God's Word will never falter, our children may still reject it, much to their detriment. Still, I believe with my whole heart that our perseverance matters. Our influence is unmatched. Our prayers are unrivaled in their devotion. And our guidance is crucial to our children's stability and confidence in going out into a world that needs their voice.

We have the opportunity, daunting though it may seem at times, to engage with a culture hungry for Truth, even while they declare it doesn't exist. And one of the best ways we can do this is by equipping our own children with the kind of solid biblical foundation that will never crack or cave to cultural pressure.

A popular recurring social media meme among conservatives for a while went something like this: "Anymore, if you want to be a rebel, you just need to get married, have lots of babies, work hard, go to church, and read your Bible." In other words, our willingness to even bring children into this world, much less commit to a lifetime investment in them, is becoming something akin to a revolutionary act.

Our willingness to even bring children into this world, much less commit to a lifetime investment in them, is becoming something akin to a revolutionary act.

In 2023, the Pew Research Center released a report showing that a record-breaking 47 percent of adults younger than fifty say they are unlikely to ever choose to have children, and the U.S. fertility rate in 2023 plummeted to 1.62 births per woman, well below the replacement rate of 2.1 births per woman.[3]

We see this trend reflected not just in numbers but in the rise in popularity of coffee mugs, stickers, and T-shirts with captions like "Proud Fur Mama" and "Plants Are Better than Humans."

And it's not a mindset restricted to secular individuals. Dr. Jeff Myers, president of Summit Ministries, a Christian apologetics camp my older children have attended multiple times, once asked me in a podcast interview what I might say to his students who claim Christ but find themselves hesitant to commit to having children, citing everything from anxiety about the state of our world to a straightforward desire to have more freedom to pursue their own interests unencumbered by the care of another human.

My answer encompassed everything from a historically Christian sexual ethic, which acknowledges the inextricable God-ordained link between sexual intimacy and procreation, to the fact that God's Word almost universally views the arrival of children as a sign of blessing and favor from the Lord. "Children are a blessing" is not the fringe battle cry of fundamentalist zealots that Reddit would have us believe. It's a simple statement of truth from the Bible, a source I'll stake my life on, all day, every day, over the clamor of worldly voices that mock the virtues of childbearing (and raising).

Because while all the "plant moms" and "dog dads" are sadly going extinct, you will be flourishing, raising kids with the goal of rooting them deeply in sound doctrine, biblical truth, godly wisdom, and a Christian mother's fierce love for the Lord and her gospel-driven compassion for the world.

Tiger Stripes of God's Grace

Regardless of how many children the Lord grants you, the mere choice to welcome them with open arms will stretch you. There's no escaping it. Remarkably, my belly bears no traditional stretch marks, even after two twin pregnancies, though my body certainly reflects other evidence of having housed and nourished my precious babies for so many years.

But if you could see my soul?

I have no doubt the tiger stripes of God's grace in allowing me to be pushed far beyond my ability to carry on in my own strength would run deep and wide. Yes, motherhood alters our bodies irrevocably. But its effects upon our hearts and minds and character—our patience, our self-reliance, our pride, our generosity (or lack thereof), our self-discipline—are infinitely more profound and lasting than any mere physical sign of sacrifice.

If you could see my soul?
I HAVE NO DOUBT THE TIGER STRIPES
OF GOD'S GRACE IN
ALLOWING ME TO BE
PUSHED FAR BEYOND
MY ABILITY TO CARRY
ON IN MY OWN
STRENGTH WOULD
RUN DEEP AND WIDE.

So take stock of the scars of grace granted you by motherhood, dear friends. Tally them lovingly alongside treasured memories of victories and even struggles that force you closer to the heart of God. Take what our culture views as blemishes (and seeks to erase) as evidence of transformation instead. For that is what it truly is. Just as with the caterpillar, the elements for our rebirth are present all along. But we must be stripped down and humbled to our very core before the Lord puts us back together, changed for the better by His Spirit, for our good and for His glory.

May your marks of motherhood ever remind you of the matchless privilege it is to be clay in our loving Potter's hands, and may we ever be ready and willing to be shaped and stretched and sculpted for His purposes.

There is nothing more "worth it" than this.

There is nothing more "worth it" than this.

The Narrative

A WORLDLY RESPONSE TO "WORTH IT"	A BIBLICAL RESPONSE TO "WORTH IT"
Perpetuates a culture of self-focus and self first	Follows Jesus's example of serving others
Views genuine exhortations and encouragement as "shaming," "judgment," or "attack"	Welcomes heartfelt constructive criticism from a biblical perspective
Resists change because it can be scary	Embraces the ways the Lord molds and shapes her to be more like Him

Action Steps

- Memorize and meditate on Philippians 2:1-2: "So if there is any encouragement in Christ, any comfort from love, any participation in the Spirit, any affection and sympathy, complete my joy by being of the same mind, having the same love, being in full accord and of one mind."
- Make a list of three areas in which motherhood has stretched and changed you the most.
- Write down three goals you have for your children (could be spiritual, practical, social, etc.).

Questions

What are some factors that you believe contribute to the uptick in self-focus and anxiety in the rising generation?

What are some practical things you could do to help your children achieve the goals you listed previously, understanding that "results" don't fully depend on your efforts?

How would you describe your attitude toward childbearing now versus when you were a teenager?

Prayer

Father, thank You for the marks of Your grace upon our hearts and souls. What a privilege to be taken apart and put back together for Your glory. May we run the race of motherhood with perseverance, trusting fully in Your sovereignty while staying committed to our God-given call to excellence and commitment. Amen.

Acknowledgments

No book exists in a vacuum, and I would be remiss if I didn't acknowledge those who helped me place this book in your hands. Jennifer, I would say you'll have to let me know if you ever get tired of editing my books for free, but I have a feeling you enjoy the exchange as much as I do. *Thank you* for your invaluable insights and expertise.

Thank you, as well, to all thirteen of the ladies whom I asked to contribute to the end of each chapter. You were my dream team, and I am so honored that every last one of you said yes. I knew this book would be enriched by your words and wisdom, and it absolutely was.

Lindsay, what a joy to watch your talents unfold in beautiful art for my books. It's such a pleasure and a privilege to work with my best friend.

Mama, you are the best mother, mentor, and Softa to my children any girl could ask for. Love you!

Heather and the team at Harvest House, thank you for your faith in me, your vision for reaching readers for Christ, and the way you treat me as family. What a gift!

Alby, you know who are and what you do. You're my favorite. Really, really.

Notes

Introduction

1. C.S. Lewis, *The Voyage of the Dawn Treader* (HarperCollins, 1952), 21.
2. Thomas O. Chisholm, "Great Is Thy Faithfulness," 1923, https://hymnary.org/text/great_is_thy_faithfulness_o_god_my_fathe.

Chapter 1: An Eternal Investment

1. R.O. Kwon, "The Parents Who Regret Having Children," *Time*, April 22, 2024, https://time.com/6966914/parental-regret-children-ro-kwon-essay/.

Chapter 2: When You Walk, Sit, Lie, and Stand

1. ABC, "Barbara Walters: Her Story (2014)," Internet Archive, May 16, 2014, https://archive.org/details/barbara-walters-her-story-2014-05-16.
2. Emily Rella, "Alexis Ohanian: Many CEOS Who Are Dads Regret This One Thing," *Entrepreneur*, August 10, 2023, https://www.entrepreneur.com/business-news/alexis-ohanian-many-ceos-who-are-dads-regret-this-one-thing/457268.

Chapter 4: It's Not Destruction, It's Development

1. Thomas Carlyle, *Sartor Resartus: The Life and Opinions of Herr Teufelsdröckh* (1833), 135, https://afterall.net/quotes/thomas-carlyle-on-irony-and-sarcasm/.
2. Thousands of my readers have already participated. Check out https://misformama.net/product/the-gentleness-challenge-ebook if you'd like more information about the challenge.
3. Craig H. Kinsley, PhD, and Elizabeth A. Meyer, "The Real 'Mommy Brain': New Mothers Grew Bigger Brains within Months of Giving Birth," American Psychological Association, accessed December 5, 2024, https://www.apa.org/news/press/releases/2010/10/mommy-brain.
4. Nicole Fabian-Weber, "10 Ways Motherhood Makes You Extraordinary, According to Science," Care.com, May 20, 2024. https://www.care.com/c/ways-motherhood-makes-you-extraordinary/.

5. Dennis Thompson, "Having More Kids Tied to Lower Odds of Alzheimer's in Women," Medical Xpress, July 24, 2018, https://medicalxpress.com/news/2018-07-kids-tied-odds-alzheimer-women.html.

6. Clare Sharp, "The Surprising Health Benefits of Pregnancy," Natural Womanhood, March 31, 2023, https://naturalwomanhood.org/health-benefits-of-pregnancy/.

7. "5 Surprising Benefits of Pregnancy," FemmPro OB/GYN & FemmPro MIDWIFE, accessed December 5, 2024, https://www.femmproobgyn.com/blog/5-surprising-benefits-of-pregnancy.

8. Abbie Halberstadt, host *M Is for Mama Podcast,* episode 63, "Passing Down the Good (A Chat with Elisha and Katie Voetberg)," podcast, April 18, 2024, https://podcasts.apple.com/us/podcast/ep-63-passing-down-the-good-a-chat-with/id1664528555?i=1000652903522.

Chapter 6: You Only Spill What's Already Inside

1. Justin Taylor, "Why Does Water Come out of the Water Bottle When It Is Shaken?" The Gospel Coalition, June 22, 2020, https://www.thegospelcoalition.org/blogs/justin-taylor/why-does-water-come-out-of-the-water-bottle-when-it-is-shaken/.

Chapter 7: When You Don't Like Them and They're Not Nice

1. Collaborative Awareness, "Speak with Kindness: How Your Words Literally Restructure Your Brain," CfCA, June 4, 2016, https://www.collaborativeawareness.com/post/2016/06/04/speak-with-kindness-how-your-words-literally-restructure-your-brain.

2. Ginger Hubbard, host, *Parenting with Ginger Hubbard*, episode 180, "Help for Children Who Bully Others," podcast, June 25, 2024, https://www.gingerhubbard.com/blogs/podcast/episode-180-help-for-children-who-bully-others.

3. Durenda Wilson, *Raising Boys to Men: A Simple, Mercifully Short Book on Raising & Homeschooling Boys* (Durenda Wilson-Simply Unhurried, 2024).

4. You can find an ebook about the Penny Reward System at https://misformama.net/product/the-penny-reward-system-ebook/.

Chapter 8: The Truth About Honest Motherhood

1. Robert Elmer, *Piercing Heaven: Prayers of the Puritans* (Lexham Press, 2022).

Chapter 10: Mothering with a Legacy Mindset

1. You can access the episode for free at www.intothelightministries.ca.

2. Register Staff, "Full Text: Harrison Butker Talks Marriage and Faith at Georgia Tech's Graduation 2023," NCR, May 29, 2024, https://www.ncregister.com/news/harrison-butker-georgia-tech-graduation-2023.

Chapter 11: What to Do When You've Grown Weary of Doing Good

1. Justin Taylor, "Do the Next Thing," The Gospel Coalition, October 25, 2017, https://www.thegospelcoalition.org/blogs/justin-taylor/do-the-next-thing/.
2. Ferris Jabr, "How Does a Caterpillar Turn into a Butterfly?" *Scientific American*, February 20, 2024, https://www.scientificamerican.com/article/caterpillar-butterfly-metamorphosis-explainer/.
3. Elizabeth Elliot, *Keep a Quiet Heart* (Fleming H. Revell, 2022).

Chapter 12: Parenting Philosophies That Aren't Worth It

1. International ALERT Academy, October 16, 2024, https://alertacademy.com/.
2. Warren Cole Smith, "Bill Gothard Resigns from Ministry," WORLD, March 7, 2014, https://wng.org/sift/bill-gothard-resigns-from-ministry-1617252154.
3. Jamie Dean, "Doug Phillips Excommunicated by Church He Founded," WORLD, November 18, 2014, https://wng.org/sift/doug-phillips-excommunicated-by-church-he-founded-1617409203.
4. Jessica Winter, "The Harsh Realm of 'Gentle Parenting,'" *The New Yorker*, March 23, 2022, https://www.newyorker.com/books/under-review/the-harsh-realm-of-gentle-parenting.
5. Bernard N. Howard, "Is 'Gentle Parenting' Biblical?" The Gospel Coalition, February 15, 2024, https://www.thegospelcoalition.org/article/gentle-parenting-biblical/.

Chapter 13: A Tiger-Striped Soul

1. Abigail Shrier, *Bad Therapy: Why the Kids Aren't Growing Up* (Sentinel, 2024).
2. Mark Manson, host, *The Subtle Art of Not Giving a F*ck*, episode 25, "How Bad Therapy Ruined a Generation (ft. Abigail Shrier)," podcast, April 10, 2024, https://markmanson.net/podcast/abigail-shrier.
3. Rachel Minkin, Juliana Menasce Horowitz, and Carolina Aragão, "The Experiences of U.S. Adults Who Don't Have Children," Pew Research Center, July 25, 2024, https://www.pewresearch.org/social-trends/2024/07/25/the-experiences-of-u-s-adults-who-dont-have-children/.

More Encouragement and Biblical Wisdom from Abbie

With biblical insight, humor, and refreshing honesty, bestselling author and mother of ten Abbie Halberstadt helps fellow moms dig deep to meet the challenges of everyday life.

misformama.com

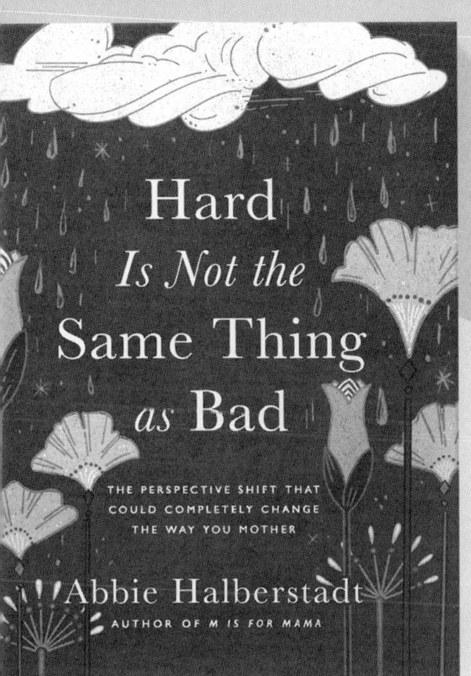
Hard
Is Not the
Same Thing
as Bad
THE PERSPECTIVE SHIFT THAT
COULD COMPLETELY CHANGE
THE WAY YOU MOTHER
Abbie Halberstadt
AUTHOR OF M IS FOR MAMA

Hard
Is Not the
Same Thing
as Bad
STUDY GUIDE
Abbie Halberstadt

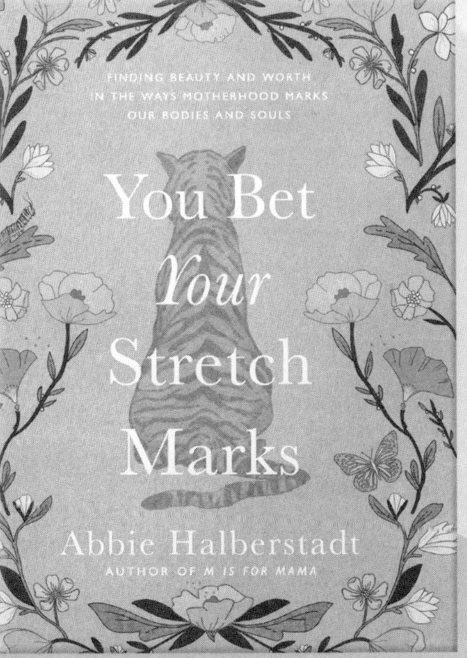
FINDING BEAUTY AND WORTH
IN THE WAYS MOTHERHOOD MARKS
OUR BODIES AND SOULS
You Bet
Your
Stretch
Marks
Abbie Halberstadt
AUTHOR OF M IS FOR MAMA

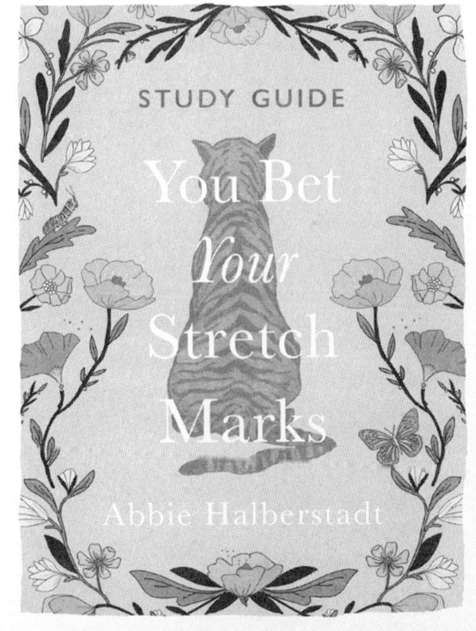
STUDY GUIDE
You Bet
Your
Stretch
Marks
Abbie Halberstadt

About the Author

Abbie Halberstadt is a happy wife and mama of ten children, including two sets of identical twins. She's also a homeschool educator, fitness instructor, business owner, speaker, writer, and pickleball enthusiast. Abbie lives by the motto that "hard is not the same thing as bad." Through her blog, podcast, and social media posts, she encourages women to dig deep to meet the challenges of everyday life. She, her husband, Shaun, and their children live in the Piney Woods of East Texas.